Management Mysterium

The Quest for Progress

BOB EMILIANI, PH.D.

Management Mysterium: The Quest for Progress / Bob Emiliani

Cover design by Bob Emiliani.

ISBN-13: 978-1-7320191-2-6
Library of Congress Control Number: 2020902803

1. Business 2. Economics 3. Management 4. Leadership 5. Spirituality

First Edition: April 2020

Published by Cubic LLC, South Kingstown, Rhode Island, USA.

This publication is believed to provide accurate information with respect to the subject matter covered. It is sold with the understanding that it does not in any way represent legal, financial, business, consulting, or other professional service.

Manufactured using digital print-on-demand technology.

CONTENTS

management *n* 1. controlling and directing the
affairs of a business or organization.

mysterium *n* 1. specialized practices unique to
an occupation or a group of people.

Preface

This is the twenty-second book that I have authored or co-authored. It is part of a larger body of writing includes nearly 50 peer-reviewed journal papers, book chapters, more than a dozen technical magazine articles, technical reports, and so on. Obviously, I love to write. I get excited about the challenge of seeing what I can produce, particularly with respect to generating and explaining new ideas that are creative, innovative, and insightful. Writing is my art. I also love to create my book covers and the images in the books to explain or feature different ideas.

What motivates my 40 years of professional writing is curiosity. This leads to study and thinking, which to me is very rewarding, and subsequently reveals itself in my writings. In retrospect, what I am most proud of is how my work has spanned three disciplines, engineering, social sciences, and humanities, across six different subject areas: leadership, management, management history, supply chain management, higher education, and materials science and engineering. I am fortunate to have had the types of employment where I could have various substantial business experiences, freely pursue my curiosities, and express my thoughts and findings in writing.

I came to the Toyota production system (TPS) and Lean 26 years ago. Within weeks of my kaizen experiences, I became a big supporter, possessing a value-laden perspective on its usefulness and benefits to people and business. Over time, my perspective has gone in the direction towards value-neutral and value-free. This came as a result of my work to understand why business leaders did not have the same value-laden perspective of Lean as I had. In pursuing this work, I had to understand business leaders' perspective, which means I had to suspend or abandon my own judgments about Lean and about them. I simply wanted to understand the "lay of the land," like a cartographer, not judge the "lay of the land." By doing this, imperfectly for sure, I believe that I have successfully, and rather comprehensively, described why business leaders have had little enthusiasm for replacing their classical management practice with Lean management.

This is the third in a series of three books. The first book, *The Triumph of Classical Management Over Lean Management: How Tradition Prevails and What to Do About It* [1], critically examined the institution of leadership. Its focus was economic, social, political historical, philosophical, and business preconceptions. It provided a comprehensive (generally materialist) analysis of why leaders resist or reject Lean management and remain committed to classical management thinking and practice.

The second book, *Irrational Institutions: Business, Its Leaders, and The Lean Movement* [2] examined the constant interplay between rational and irrational thinking that occurs in business, their fundamental importance and necessity in human thinking and problem-solving, and how they inform management decision-making for better or worse. Importantly, it showed how aesthetic judgments contribute to making business, its leaders, and the Lean movement captive to the status quo of classical management.

Management Mysterium: The Quest for Progress looks at a mostly invisible aspect of management practice: the intangible spiritual, sacred, and the sometimes mysterious and mythical aspects of managing organizations. It is the realm of the nonmaterial; the spiritual and mental forces that guide one's thinking and which results in maintaining the status quo or which results in breaking the status quo. The nonphysical world is the place where beliefs and assumptions uncritically accepted true are passed from one generation to another. These play an important role in the basic functioning of business as it is expressed by management thinking and practice. For it is within this realm where the facts (see Note 1) – the truth – of a matter can be unconvincing given the things that people believe in. In other words, secular spiritual beliefs can easily override facts and the need for improvement, thus leading to long-term stagnation.

This book was a different challenge for me because it crosses many boundaries and examines a delicate subject, spirituality and its transformation from Christianity to the secular world of business through the field of economics. More specifically, the secular world of management, which continuously intersects with the practice of leadership. This book, like the other two, examines the question of why most leaders resist or reject progressive new systems of management such as Lean management. Leaders' rejection of progressive management is nothing new; its history dates to the early 1900s. But until my work, people had nothing more than a superficial understanding of why this occurred. That level of understanding cannot continue if progressive management is to gain a larger and stronger footing.

The three books examine this complex problem, why most leaders resist or reject Lean management, from different directions (Figure P-1). The primary purpose is to obtain a

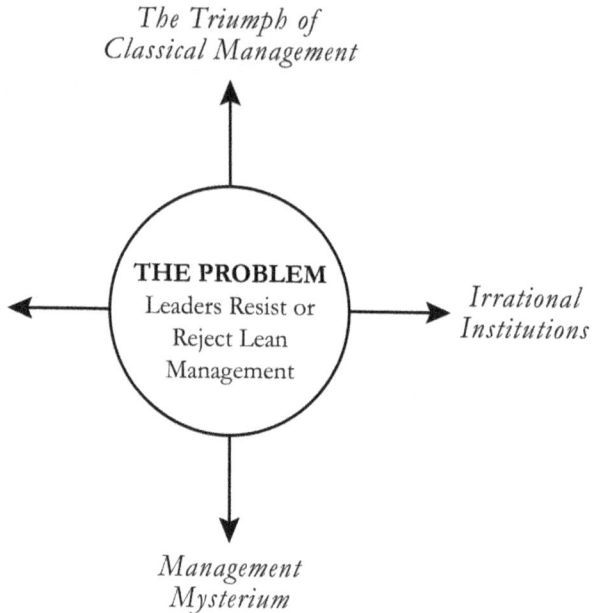

The Triumph of
Classical Management

THE PROBLEM
Leaders Resist or
Reject Lean
Management

Irrational
Institutions

Management
Mysterium

Figure P-1. Analysis of the problem from different directions.

more complete picture of the problem so that a larger set of countermeasures can be identified and implemented to advance the spread of progressive Lean management (see Note 2). A secondary purpose is to improve people's literacy in the hermetic ways of leaders. Meaning, to understand how leaders think and to understand why they do what they do, or not do, in their work managing organizations. The books deconstruct leadership so that people can obtain clear understanding of what goes on at work and why. People might not like what they learn, but they will feel a calmness in finally knowing the mindset of leaders, why leaders do what they do, and whose interests they serve.

The books are based in part on my direct personal experience with both classical management and Lean management, wherein the former is clearly deficient compared to the latter given its archaic foundations and the needs of business and society for the last 75 years and into the future. The three directions I have examined cover the main locus of my curiosities: the institution of leadership, reason and aesthetics, and secular spirituality in management and leadership practice. Is there a fourth direction from which to examine this problem? Indeed, there is, and I believe it is the legal preconceptions, from Roman law to English common law to present-day law – a subject that others are better suited than I to write about (see Note 3).

Figure P-2 appeared in the Preface of *Irrational Institutions*. It is reproduced again here because of its significance to the topics covered in *Management Mysterium*. Dr. W. Edwards Deming created the "System of Profound Knowledge" [3] (SoPK) whose purpose was to overcome the status quo and enable progress in organizations (see Note 4). My graphical depiction of the "System of Profound Knowledge" is shown on the left side. In SoPK, humans are at the forefront and leaders are enablers of progress. Select people from the underlying population pass through the small hole at the bottom to lead the progress of humanity through its ever-changing circumstances. Humans utilize their natural senses and abilities to learn and solve problems so that they can advance as times and needs dictate.

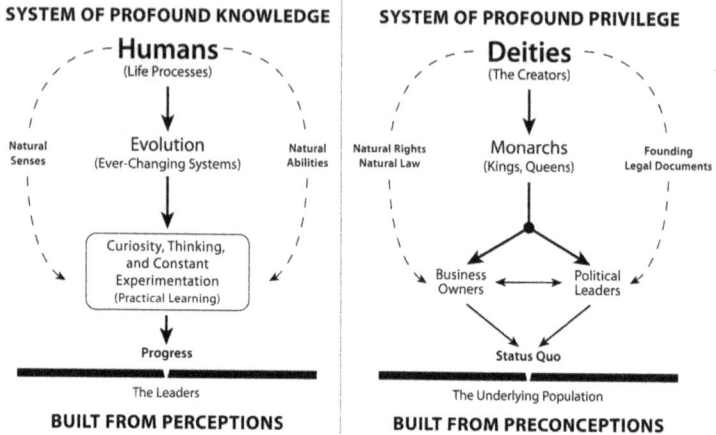

SYSTEM OF PROFOUND KNOWLEDGE

Humans
(Life Processes)

Natural Senses

Evolution
(Ever-Changing Systems)

Natural Abilities

Curiosity, Thinking, and Constant Experimentation
(Practical Learning)

Progress

The Leaders

BUILT FROM PERCEPTIONS

SYSTEM OF PROFOUND PRIVILEGE

Deities
(The Creators)

Natural Rights
Natural Law

Monarchs
(Kings, Queens)

Founding Legal Documents

Business Owners ⟷ Political Leaders

Status Quo

The Underlying Population

BUILT FROM PRECONCEPTIONS

Figure P-2. In SoPK, humans are at the forefront and leaders are enablers. In SoPP leaders are descended from deities. SoPK is built from human sensory perceptions while SoPP is built from preconceptions.

My study of the institution of leadership reveals the existing system and its remarkable effectiveness at obstructing progress, which Dr. Deming recognized. The right side of Figure P-2 shows the long-established system, the "System of Profound Privilege" (SoPP). In SoPP, leaders are at the forefront while the underlying population serves a functional role. Leaders draw select people up from the underlying population to support their business or political interests and to help maintain the status quo. The fundamental purpose of SoPP is to obstruct progress or assure that progress does not proceed so quickly as to compromise the rights and privileges of the vested interests.

Importantly, SoPK – like TPS and Lean management – is built from human sensory perceptions while SoPP – classical management – is built from preconceptions of how organizations (and society) should be structured and how and when power should be used. The focus of SoPK is human survival and there is little concern about privilege. Progress is more important than privilege. Progress comes into being through productive workmanship. The focus of SoPP is privilege and assumes that human survival is a given. Status quo is more important than concern for survival. Status quo comes into being through salesmanship. This book will explore these dichotomies and how secular spirituality (see Note 5) in business and management descended from Christianity through the field of economics.

I hope *Management Mysterium* proves to be an informative and worthwhile contribution, and that it successfully rounds-out the series of three books focused on this problem – a problem that applies to more than just Lean management. The books are broadly applicable to understanding why major organizational changes are so difficult to achieve. Through such understanding may come progress.

Bob Emiliani
South Kingstown, Rhode Island
April 2020

Questions to Reflect On

- In Figure P-2, SoPP (classical management) clearly suggests that wealth and power are unearned, divorced from the human propensity for both productive and efficient work. SoPK (Lean management) suggests the opposite, but not quite so because wealth and power are more fairly distributed from top to bottom. Be truthful: If you were a beneficiary of SoPP and became wealthy and powerful (top 0.1% or better), would you think or do any differently than your peer group or your betters? Would you really be interested in Lean management? For what reasons? Would you be interested in democratizing work and wealth? If yes, why? If no, why not?

- In Figure P-2, SoPP represents the status quo. Challenges to that by SoPK face significant resistance, including the invocation of myriad difficulties, upset, and harshly unfavorable outcomes. The talkers and writers will come out in force for as long as it takes to confuse and mystify the public and submerge the "progressive collectivist agenda" (a pejorative characterization of Lean). How should the Lean community fight that, to liberate humanity from SoPP (classical management)? Identify ten methods.

- In Figure P-2, SoPK clearly suggests that no person at any level of an organization should be blind to rational scientific thinking. That's not to say that there is not generous space for irrational thinking and secular spirituality as these too are part of human information processing. Why does SoPP work so hard to hide the facts from self? And from others?

Notes

1. Where facts are understood to be impersonal or inert objects, not something that possesses a spiritual (animistic) essence or power which can impart a force on or external threat to humans. The importance of this distinction will become apparent in subsequent pages.

2. Lean management is understood to be a close replica of Toyota's management system; e.g., see Emiliani, B. *et al.* (2007), *Better Thinking, Better Results: Case Study and Analysis of an Enterprise-Wide Lean Transformation*, second edition, The CLBM, LLC, Wethersfield, Conn.

3. Presumably, there is also a neurological basis for leaders resisting or rejecting Lean management. Brain imaging could reveal the preference for classical management by showing subjects (presidents and CEOs) appropriate imagery related to tradition, power, wealth, sentimentality, and attachment. The resulting images may reveal the parts of the brain that most strongly resist or reject Lean management.

4. In this and the two related books, *The Triumph of Classical Management* and *Irrational Institutions*, progress means to make changes based on needs more-or-less as they become apparent, in order to keep up with the times and with the evolution of humanity so that people and social organizations to not fall into arrears. Social organizations that increasingly fall behind the times will fail to meet the expectations and needs of people, resulting in multiform

distress that could otherwise be avoided. The changes needed to make sensorially identifiable progress are neither radical nor cosmetic. Rather, they are continuous ameliorative adjustments, sometimes large and most other times small, made when needed, and to avoid the need for large periodic (sudden) changes which are disruptive, more difficult to manage, and invariably produce poor results. This description of progress, morally and ethically erect in its intention, is not a description of pragmatism which is most often used to keep things very close to what they currently are and may therefore be morally and ethically deficient. There is also the recognition that people make mistakes or that progress can produce unintended outcomes. In such cases, the solution is not to retreat or abandon the means and methods of progress, but to make corrections more-or-less in the time that they are needed so as to avoid the stultifying grip of the status quo and subordination of human ingenuity. Embedded in this description is an admittedly value-laden judgment as to the beneficent nature of continuous ameliorative adjustments (i.e. progress) when performed adeptly and with alacrity.

5. Secular spirituality is defined as: "the adherence to a spiritual philosophy without adherence to a religion" (source: https://en.wikipedia.org/wiki/Secular_spirituality). In *Management Mysterium*, secular spirituality means the human spirituality associated with the material world.

References

[1] Emiliani, B. (2018), *The Triumph of Classical Management Over Lean Management: How Tradition Prevails and What to Do About It*, Cubic, LLC, South Kingstown, Rhode Island

[2] Emiliani, B. (2020), *Irrational Institutions: Business, Its Leaders, and The Lean Movement*, Cubic, LLC, South Kingstown, Rhode Island

[3] Deming, W. (1994), *The New Economics: For Industry, Government, Education*, Second Edition, Chapter 4, The W. Edwards Deming Institute, Ketchum, Idaho

"The immediate, direct effect of the animistic habit of thought upon the general frame of mind of the believer goes in the direction of lowering his effective intelligence in the respect in which intelligence is of especial consequence for modern industry."

– Thorstein Veblen

Introduction

This book, and the two earlier books *The Triumph of Classical Management Over Lean Management: How Tradition Prevails and What to Do About It* and *Irrational Institutions: Business, Its Leaders, and The Lean Movement*, are focused on understanding why the quest for progress in the practice of management has been so difficult. Over the years, thousands of people have put extraordinary effort into trying to get business leaders to recognize the limitations of classical management and recognize the benefits of progressive management – the current form of which is Lean management. While there have been some noticeable successes, the overall result is disappointing. Lean may be a superior management system and way of thinking, but it continues to lose big to classical management and traditional ways of thinking. When people who have been trained in Lean management reach the highest levels of an organization, they almost always succumb to classical management. As my work has shown, there is no single cause for these observed effects. The enduring nature of classical management suggests that there are aspects of it that operate beyond the level of consciousness – something at the unconscious level of one's beliefs. In particular, spirituality, whose origins are both religious and secular. This book briefly examines religious spirituality, with the far greater emphasis being secular spirituality.

Spirituality is part of every person's life whether one is religious, agnostic, or atheist. Humans believe in things in good times or bad. Beliefs are part of how we think and how we try to understand our world through the continuous interplay between rational and irrational thinking. Humans have enough intelligence to understand many things, but not all things. The things we do not understand at any point in time are typically consigned to the spiritual realm. This is both a necessary and useful part of how humans process information. It brings closure to that which we do not understand, that which we care not to understand, or that which we perceive as not worth understanding. It provides a sense of certainty in unpredictable situations. It relieves anxiety and allows us to move on to other matters of importance.

When a good thing happens, we say we are "lucky," "fortunate," or "blessed." What we actually mean is that we do not fully understand how or why we were the recipient of that good thing that happened. Lucky, fortunate, or blessed are shorthand for saying "I don't know." When a bad thing happens, we say were "unlucky," "unfortunate," or "cursed." What we actually mean is that we do not fully understand how or why we were the recipient of that bad thing that happened. Unlucky, unfortunate, or cursed are also shorthand for saying "I don't know." Even if we know with certainty the cause of the good or bad thing that happened, we may still think that good or bad luck had something to do with it. This could be, simply, an attribution common to a society or culture. Nevertheless, it reflects a spiritual belief that is unique to human beings.

Things happen to people such as:

You have managed to avoid serious illness or injury. Was it due to mother's care, vaccinations, healthy diet, choices made, or risk avoidance?

You bought a lottery ticket and won $500. Was is because you are good at picking lottery tickets, because you went to your usual lottery retailer, or because the seller unexpectedly directed you to a new lottery game?

You were in a car accident. Was it bad timing, the result of an unplanned detour, or was it due to an inexperienced driver?

A big tree fell in a storm, landed on your house, and caused major damage. Was it due to carpenter ants, the wind direction, drought, or poor tree maintenance?

Whatever the actual cause or causes may be, people are certain to attribute some portion of these personal events to good or bad luck.

In business, things happen that people often attribute to good luck or bad luck:

The company has been exceeding performance expectations in all areas for the last six quarters. Was it due to the release of pent-up demand, great salesmanship, flawless execution, or favorable terms of sale?

You beat several other qualified people for a big promotion. Was it because people like you, a boss who hires in their image, the color of your skin, or your strong track record of accomplishments?

You got laid off from your job. Was it due to management over-hiring, outsourcing, poor work quality, investors demanding higher returns, or poor cost control?

Your department did not meet its quota for the quarter. Was it due to a slackening of demand, poor salesmanship, the weather, poorly targeted advertising, or ineffective sales incentives?

Likewise, whatever the actual cause or causes may be, people are certain to attribute some portion of business events to good or bad luck.

As described here, good luck, bad luck, and so on are expressions of superstition: beliefs that are not based on knowledge or reason. Again, we often lack the knowledge to understand things and may lack the interest or ability to apply reasoning to events that have transpired. Spirituality and superstition will be found in life and in business – management and leadership of organizations, where intelligence and rational thinking are prized. Superstitions, primitive in origin (limbic system of the brain), are part of the structure of social systems and have no trouble surviving through time. Because superstitions are effective at ameliorating fear and anxiety, they take on the appearance of being grounded in objective reality.

Whether in life or business, there exists levels of complexity and complex combinations of things going on that we do not understand but are compelled to find ways, however weak or strong, to explain what happened. And because thinking is difficult to do – e.g. rigorous analysis of cause and effect – we typically pick simplistic answers (see Note 1). We have heard simplistic answers from other people and so we repeat them, and we assume people will continue to accept them – even in cases where there are substantial consequences for the failure to comprehend cause and effect. Additionally, simplistic answers give managers a feeling of accomplishment, which registers in the brain as a release of dopamine and frees them to move on to something else.

Evidence of the existence of secular spirituality and superstition is simplistic solutions to complex problems. For example, the management of a large-scale organization is a difficult challenge. There is a lot going on that no CEO can fully understand. When financial results lag, the simplistic solution is invariably to lay people off, close offices and plant sites, and squeeze suppliers for lower prices. Small-scale organizations also present difficult challenges for the top leader. The perpetually changing conditions that exists in business – chaos and uncertainty – direct management decision-making towards certain rules-of-thumb or intuitive judgments based on experience that are difficult to call into question. Managers' bias towards success and against failure results in confidence in one's abilities and the assumed effectiveness of simplistic solutions. These beliefs are superstitions that have great influence in determining the perceived (favorable) value of managerial competence and effectiveness. But is that warranted?

Managers establish plans that they expect others lower in the hierarchy to execute. But, unable to predict the future, managers *hope* that the plan is achievable and *hope* that others will execute the plan as managers *envision* it. They *expect* there will be no impediments. Managers have *confidence* in the ability of people to get the job done and *envision* success. Managers have *faith* in their *forecasts* and *predictions*. In this way, superstitions exist in business as prophecies (foretelling future events) with respect to plans, projects, budgets, and the like, and their execution – the general conduct of business and management decision-making.

The invocation of superstition in business is unavoidable and perhaps not even wrong, but it becomes wrong when superstition is invoked as an excuse (simplistic solution) for common problems such as when people are blamed and made to suffer due to failures in processes, as measured by a metric or key performance indicator (KPI). Managers who blame people for process problems anthropomorphize natural phenomena – random variation in a process (see Note 2). Doing so introduces a mythology useful to managers, easily made viral and difficult to extinguish, that people are the problem. This superstition, like others, are transmitted by managers from one generation to next.

Figure I-1 shows an example of anthropomorphizing natural phenomena. Metrics and KPIs are non-human. The favorability or unfavorability of the metric or KPI is ascribed to a person. The person is praised if the metric is favorable and blamed if it is unfavorable. Either way, the metric has been anthropomorphized (see Note 3).

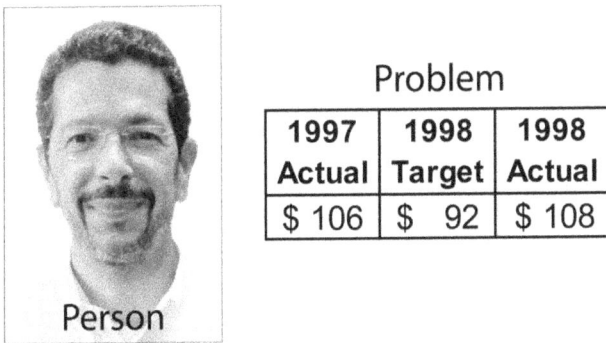

Problem

1997 Actual	1998 Target	1998 Actual
$ 106	$ 92	$ 108

Person

Figure I-1. The metric is the apparent problem while the person is the actual problem. People get blamed for bad processes that cannot produce the desired result (1998 target, in millions).

Superstitions are embedded in assumptions that exist in the background, but they come to the surface in language such as "My *belief* is," "I *think*," "It *feels* to me like," and "I *fear.*" They shape how we think, at times more irrational than rational, and become generalized rules that are broadly recognized as sufficient for answering a question or solving a problem. Superstitions anchor us to the past because they inhibit the motivation and curiosity needed to understand or improve our understanding of causality.

Spirituality, and associated superstition, is normally thought to be a good thing in that it can explain good outcomes. It can even be part of how one achieves a good outcome, such as having a positive team spirit to take on a seemingly impossible challenge. But spirituality and superstition can also be disempowering. It can impel people to surrender to the status quo and result in the obstruction or retardation of needed progress. This occurs when people are unable or unwilling to determine the facts of the matter. One can always do more to determine the facts of the matter. Usually, that means detailed root cause analysis. However, rigorous analytical methods are normally reserved for major failures, though sometimes not even for that. Instead, people revert to simplistic answers to the cause of problems – e.g. the problem was caused by a few bad apples, the weather, customer defections, and so on Spirituality and associated superstition are an important part of our belief system, and partly embody what it means to be human. They are incorporated into all aspects of life, including work, whether one realizes it or not.

For all the focus on rational, data-driven decision-making over the last 40 years, secular spirituality and superstition remain important components of management thinking and decision-making. This brings the central problem that this book examines into focus: uncritical acceptance, which means to accept something without asking any questions. When this occurs, there is an acceptance of a spiritual or magical or supernatural belief. Preconceptions are treated as something that is true, and thus there is no need to ask questions.

Uncritical acceptance can, and most frequently does, obstruct needed progress in the practice of management and leadership, which, in turn, obstructs needed progress in society. Uncritical acceptance keeps managers stuck in the past and wedded to outdated traditions, which makes them unreceptive to learning. Employees, in particular, dislike managers whose decision-making is weak on facts and poor in consideration for people and their workplace needs.

Most managers, regardless of their level in the organization, have no formal job requirement to perform rigorous problem-solving on one problem per year, twice a year, four times a year, 12 times a year, 24 times a year, 48 times a year, or more. Instead, on-the-job management training consists of the rapid absorption of simplistic solutions rooted in the spiritual and supernatural that have been learned from one's superiors. The System of Profound Privilege allows this to occur and to continue indefinitely. It is a privilege reserved for the leaders of organizations, while workers are required to understand cause and effect in their work.

The System of Profound Privilege is built from the sum of numerous preconceptions that exist within each of the eight categories shown in Figure I-2. This is what makes change such a difficult problem. If you can demolish preconceptions in one category, there remain numerous preconceptions in each of the remaining seven categories [1]. The sum of all preconceptions succeeds at retarding progress – but not in every organization. Toyota has long had a management development system whereby managers coach subordinates, coupled with hands-on work   to

$$\sum$$ Economic
Social
Political
Historical
Philosophical
Legal
Business
Spiritual

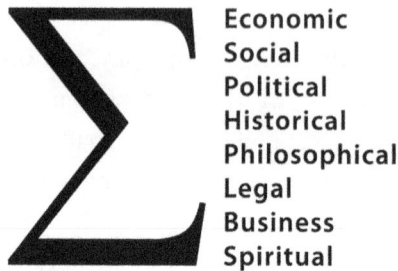

Figure I-2. The sum of preconceptions in the eight categories poses a formidable challenge. Each category contains numerous preconceptions that derail efforts to develop people and improve processes, which results in the status quo.

improve sensory perceptions and promotion from within, to methodically eliminate many of the interconnected preconceptions over time and to allow the emergence and sustainment of something akin to Dr. Deming's System of Profound Knowledge [2]. This management development system replaces "My *belief* is," "I *think*," "It *feels* to me like," and "I *fear*" with "I *observed*," "I *studied*," "I've *learned*," and, ultimately, "The *facts* are." Facts democratize knowledge and destroys or diminishes certain leadership rights and privileges that are held dear in classical management (see Note 4). It should be no surprise that within this progressive management practice, there also exists many spiritual beliefs, as will be discussed in subsequent pages.

As we proceed further in this book, it is important to understand that no value judgment is made with respect to religious or secular spirituality. It examines these two forms of spirituality in business, with the main focus on secular spirituality; human spirituality associated with the material world. Chapter 1, "The New Religion: Economics," examines Christian morality and ethics in medieval European Church teachings about money and trade, and how some of these teachings remain with us today in our understanding of economics and the practice of management. It illuminates the historical interest the Church had in economic matters in relation to social obligations and the desire to maintain strict order in society.

Chapter 2, "Classical Management Spirituality," examines secular spirituality in business, how it is used, how this informs management thinking and practice, and what it achieves. Chapter 3, "Lean Management Spirituality" examines secular spirituality in the practice of Lean management and how it differs from secular spirituality in classical management. There is also a brief examination of how secular spirituality manifests itself in the Lean movement.

Finally, various terms are used to describe those responsible for putting leadership and the system of management practice into action. The terms CEO, top leader, leader, senior manager, manager, and management team are used to denote the top leader or chain of command, from CEO to supervisor. Their meaning in context should be obvious to the reader.

Questions to Reflect On

- How does secular spirituality manifest itself in your management practice?
- Which superstitions do you use or rely on in your management practice?
- Can you think of examples where simplistic solutions led to the avoidance of problem-solving?
- Can you think of examples where simplistic solutions obscured the root cause of an important problem?
- Can you think two or three examples of uncritical acceptance that impede your performance as a manager?
- Can you think two or three examples of uncritical acceptance that impede performance of your department or company?

Notes

1. Simplistic solutions differ from simple solutions. The former means to treat complex problems with excessive or unrealistic simplicity (oversimplification), while the latter means solutions that are uncomplicated, easy to understand, or modest. For complex problems, simple, elegant solutions are superior to simplistic solutions.

2. Perhaps someday workers will shout to their boss, "Don't anthropomorphize me," to force recognition of the need for structured problem-solving to determine the root cause(s) of problems.

3. Top leaders nearly always attribute business problems to external objects or events. These are seen by leaders as the honest   and   true   force(s)   of   misfortune. Anthropomorphizing is done for the purpose of blame-shifting, and thus to maintain one's status, rights, and privileges. This is a far lesser sin than to publicly admit one's shortcomings. The exception being force majeure (act of God), as, for example, with the COVID-19 virus. But even within the context of a pandemic, one can make an easy claim of corporate mismanagement by top leaders. For example, the leaders of large corporations, unceasingly success oriented and money-focused, thought it wise to spend huge sums of money over the last decade buying back shares of their own stock, usually at inflated prices, rather than saving money so as to be able to survive a major downturn or crisis. Industry regular succumbs to some large problem, typically every seven to 10 years in the form of the

business cycle (recession), high energy prices, shortages of material, etc. Instead of saving money for business continuity (e.g. three to six months of operating expense), money earned was spent unwisely on stock buybacks (e.g. Boeing), in a herd mentality, with company leaders betting that the money will not someday be needed. Instead, the pandemic forced leaders to rely on taxpayers for business survival. Cash-to-debt ratios of 0.1 to 0.2 are insufficient to survive a crisis. Also note the vast sums of money wasted on executive compensation over the last 30 years under the superstition that remuneration is based on competence; that reward is commensurate with work. With the façade now gone and the magic revealed, claims made as to top leaders' pecuniary value to the corporation was never valid. This and other forms of corporate mismanagement can be easily recognized in this book as well as *The Triumph of Classical Management* and *Irrational Institutions*.

4. Facts also change relationships between people. A group or social network that possesses a certain belief system does not desire to have it disrupted by the facts. Not only does it upset one's assumptions about how things work or should work, the strain it places on personal relationships serves as a disincentive to acknowledge the facts. Acknowledging the facts requires one to join or develop a new social network (ideological and political) and accept being ostracized from their long-established social network. Both are outcomes that most people wish to avoid. This helps explain why it has been so difficult to expand membership in the Lean movement among those of high social status (senior corporate leaders) as well as the working class.

References

[1] Emiliani, B. (2018), *The Triumph of Classical Management Over Lean Management: How Tradition Prevails and What to Do About It*, Cubic, LLC, South Kingstown, Rhode Island

[2] Deming, W. (1994), *The New Economics: For Industry, Government, Education*, Second Edition, Chapter 4, The W. Edwards Deming Institute, Ketchum, Idaho

1
The New Religion: Economics

"...embedded in this early-modern system are large remnants which have stood over from antiquity and from the Middle Ages; as how should it not, since it is in all its constituents a creature of habit and tradition?"

.
.
.

"As a matter of course very much of the institutional furniture of the Middle Ages has stood over and has continued to govern men's conduct and convictions very nicely in one bearing and another through the modern era."

- Thorstein Veblen

The New Religion: Economics

This chapter is a short summary of a critical period, the high and late Middle Ages in Europe (ca. 1100-1700), that laid the foundation for separating the economic interests of the Roman Catholic Church from the economic interests of the State and the individual [1-3]. During this period, there was a remarkable change in both factual understanding and beliefs about individuals and their capability to chart their own life experience free of comprehensive religious authority. The catalyst was a change in sentiment about the usefulness of the restrictions placed by the Church on trade. Reason – asking questions – became more appealing than compliance to religious authority. Trade in society became more desired and more necessary than revelation. This change was centuries in the making and truly revolutionary, but, centuries later, it ended up producing its own forms of secularized status quo from the residue of 17th century religious beliefs.

The basis for this change was the explication of humanity in terms of Natural Rights (rights of life, liberty, and property [see Note 1]) derived from the laws of Nature, as described by 17th century Enlightenment philosophers Thomas Hobbes and John Locke. This gave the State sanction to become the authority on matters that were previously the province of the Church. Thus, in certain affairs of human life, the supernatural gave way to the human individual, with rights conferred by Nature – property rights, equality, individual freedom, freedom of contract, etc. Society's existence shifts from a solely religious explanation to one that is rooted in Nature, resulting in the secularization of society and various activities, especially trade. The role of the State was to provide a guiding hand toward prosperity through the protection of private property and the enforcement of contracts. These changes were due to practical necessities as society grew and evolved, and as human wants and needs changed (Figure 1-1).

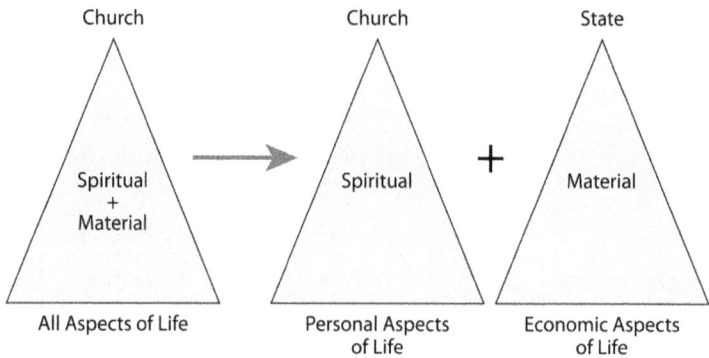

Figure 1-1. In the early Middle Ages, the Church was the ultimate authority over all aspects of life and society. By the late Middle Ages, the spiritual and material worlds began to separate, with the Church being the ultimate authority over personal life and the State being the ultimate authority over economic aspects of life (the individual and joint-stock corporation) as well as law.

The separation occurred slowly over time and was never complete, then or now. The material world was de-spiritualized and incorporated into the State and society, yet there remain areas of overlap or connection between the spiritual and material worlds, either implicitly or explicitly. Today's business world, as we shall soon see, has ties to Medieval Christian spirituality and developed its own separate and unique secular spirituality.

Medieval society was unequal, precisely ordered and graded into various classes with well-defined status and functions: the priesthood, nobility, landlords, military, merchants, money lenders, craftsmen, and peasants working the fields. Inequality between classes was seen as necessary for the feudal system to function effectively and maintain a submissive and peaceful society. People born into their rank spent their lifetime in that rank. Making "all men equal" was contrary to God's will and degraded the spiritual foundation of society.

Traditional Church teaching viewed commerce as subordinate to human life – meaning, salvation. Trade between people was subject to the moral teachings of the church, and coincident with personal conduct because trade tempts humans with pecuniary gain in the same way that humans are tempted in other ways. Trade and wealth were viewed as legitimate by the Church. However, wealth should be no more than that which is necessary for living (sustenance) and the need for survival given one's occupation in Medieval society. Importantly, both trade and wealth must benefit the public. Trade must be carried on with just (fair) prices so as not to grind down the poor, and the proper, moral use of wealth was for charity to help the poor and the needy. Christian charity was an accepted obligation, especially among the wealthy. The Church taught that prices should be the cost of material (if applicable) and one's labor, and no more. Private property was seen as necessary to avoid quarrels and conflict over common property, but also evil because of the temptation to build wealth for one's self. Avarice, the pursuit of money or material gain, was immoral. The life of the laborer and craftsman was admirable because they were largely untouched by the sin of avarice, unlike the money lenders or merchants who constantly succumbed to temptation.

The merchant who "buys cheap and sells dear" and who is unconcerned with Christian charity is condemned for his actions. Economic immorality upsets social stability. Therefore, personal morality overrides economic expediency. The Church teachings on the morality and ethics of trade and money sought to prevent social unrest in society by denouncing usurers, people who withhold payment of wages, cheat when selling (short weights or measures), sell at high prices to unsuspecting buyers, raise prices when supply is scarce, landlords who constantly raise rents, and the like. Usurers were refused sacrament, absolution, and Christian burial, and subject to Church trials and harsh penalties. Middlemen were seen as parasites, not men of virtue. Through its teachings, the Church controlled and suppressed economic activity to ensure its conformance to personal morals and that society would remain committed to religious foundations. Economic activity must serve society, not be the master of society. Economic transactions made within the strict moral teachings of the Church assured the type of stable social relations that both the Church and State sought.

In the Medieval Age, usury meant any type of trade that was unfair to the weaker party; engaging in sharp, unChristian dealing, or having an unmerciful heart driven towards individual pecuniary gain. Usury and other forms of moral and ethical delinquency was an easy way to find fault with people and punish them to control society and thus maintain the Church's influence and enforce its teachings to assure moral rectitude in trade and financial matters. If interest was to be charged, it had to be 10 percent or less and people could not be forced into contract. They had to do so freely as commerce was tied to the common interest. Violators of Christian morals – perjury, fraud, extortion, usury, short weights and measures, high prices, high interest rates – were subject to excommunication. If a trader lost money, it was their own fault. One's losses could not be covered by charging higher prices to future buyers. It was more important to avoid sin than to avoid loss. In the hierarchy of human values, economic affairs ranked far below religious and civic values.

While Church teaching had long been against capital and credit, over time these came to be seen as indispensable to society and so Church teachings were no longer relevant. Social and economic conditions had changed over the centuries and the conditions under which Christian morality and ethics were established were either fading or no longer existed. The Church, like any individual or organization, struggled to understand when changes in society render traditions to be no longer useful. Renaissance-era commercial transactions from the great centers of finance and trade (Italy, Netherlands, Spain) became more widely accepted practice when they were conducted in service to God and in pursuit of a Christian life. People engaged in commerce, the Church, and the State, being in conflict with one another, take what would later become known as a *laissez faire* ("let [it] go") approach to economic transactions. Along with these changes comes other changes in sentiment. Ecclesiastical discipline (e.g. trials, excommunication) begins to lose its preventative effect and becomes less credible as a means for controlling society. Common law courts, and the Monarch as enforcer of law, grew to resent the encroachment of ecclesiastical courts in conducting civil trials and administering punishments. Within a century (ca. 1570-1670), excessive pecuniary gain went from being contrary to God's law to being congruent with the laws of Nature (i.e. Natural Rights of mankind).

Christian charity went from an obligation to give to the poor to requiring the poor to work for their bread. Almsgiving was Christian charity gone awry. Poverty was not the fault of society; it was the fault of the poor or needy and a direct consequence of their idleness – proof of personal demerit. Charity does not provide relief; it furthers dependence. Work became revered while idleness and poverty were scorned. Don't pamper the poor; make them earn their wages through work. But, never pay the poor too much because they will waste their wages on drink, gambling, prostitution, fortune telling, and other vices. It was seen as self-evident that one should keep the lower classes poor to assure that they have the incentive to remain industrious and correct their moral failings and affections for debauchery.

Labor was God-like, a virtue that is good for both the mind and body, while idleness was socially evil and a sin. Disentanglement of social and economic affairs from religious and political affairs meant the Church was no longer the ultimate authority in determining the morality of public and private life. The state became the ultimate authority, with sanction from the Church.

Centuries-old feudal society, with its ordered and graded classes, hierarchy of status, mutual obligations, and the Church's enforcement of personal morality, finally began to fracture. Social stability, long prized by both Church and State, was forced to relinquish the status-quo and adapt to the new reality. Yet both maintain important elements of power and tradition to minimize their losses and position themselves for the possibility of future gain. Society was slowly turning from religious interests towards commercial interests, where individualism and economic growth, once seen as life-sapping and now turned life-giving. Piety was losing in the competition for ideas on how humans should interact with one another and for whom they should be held accountable to jointly or severally. Private gain would expand opportunity and produce a better life for citizens and position the state as the ultimate authority, thus eclipsing the historical domain of the Church as the master of trade and economic morality.

The old phrase "trade is one thing, religion is another" captures the growing sentiment of the New Religion: economic self-interest. This was argued to be congruent with God's plan, and in doing so maintained a connection to God but not necessarily the Church itself. This was a sufficiently strong spiritual connection so that the Church could not make the claim that economic self-interest was devoid of all moral character or supernatural association. There is no conflict between spiritual and secular callings. The glory of God and mundane materialism can coexist. The Church's instinctive conservatism means self-protection in times of great change. Its acquiescence illustrates awareness that society's demand for change must, eventually, proceed, as these basic human desires cannot be suppressed.

Society was not content with the satisfaction of basic survival needs of food, clothing, and shelter. Ascetic life and consumption congruent with antiquated and superstitious Church teachings of immoral behavior and social vices fell out of favor. Society demanded individual freedoms, expanded commerce, and prosperity. One's labor in economic enterprise was successfully argued to be in the service of God. The sins of self-interest and pecuniary gain were converted into a virtue. The change in standard, from serving one master, God, to two, God and economic enterprise, enabled the growth of economic activity to be seen as a moral duty. Faith, the Christian motif, became part of the solid foundation for commerce, no longer its quicksand. Property became a right ahead of the rights of the Church and State, thus allowing the pursuit of economic self-interest.

The work of political economists Adam Smith and Thomas Malthus, and later David Ricardo and John Stuart Mill, take what came before them (e.g. Hobbes, Locke, Rousseau) and put it into a fully coherent moral and economic philosophy Called "liberal economic model," or more commonly, "liberalism" (see Note 2). The New Religion came into being through a slow drift of change occurring in society over the course of hundreds of years, punctuated by revolutionary thinking and disruptive events – the Age of Enlightenment and the Reformation. Both slow drift and new disruptions were necessary to give the New Religion its life. It is through this process that society was compelled to think and do things differently. The changes were absorbed by the secular realm and became part of the everyday habit of thinking and practice.

The authoring of books on political economy and the teaching of economics in 19th century universities was by Doctor of Divinity degree-holders, practicing clergymen, and others closely affiliated with the Protestant religion [4]. The New Religion, economic liberalism – Natural Rights, property, freedom of contract – became globally influential in the 19th and 20th centuries. This occurred through various processes including formal education, emulation, and social learning. Over time, liberalism becomes a common and influential way of secular thinking regardless of one's personal religion or the source of that common way of thinking. The New Religion, economics, as we understand it today, is largely a product of this intertwined religious and social history (see Notes 2 and 3).

Many elements of this short outline of the religious and social conditions in the high and late Middle Ages in Europe (ca. 1100-1700) should be familiar to readers today in relation to the common understanding of religion, social values and sentiments, and economics. The salient point being that, in varying types and degrees, the spiritual past is ever-present. We still talk about Adam Smith's "invisible hand," a clear reference to the presence of a supernatural force in free markets. We still talk about *laissez faire* as the preferred way for markets to operate, unencumbered by the state or religious organization. We still talk about how a market economy (the "magic" of markets) is the most efficient way to allocate resources. And we still talk about how an individual satisfying their own economic interest accrues to benefit the community and society at-large. While economics has evolved and expanded since the 18th century, it retains some of the thinking of its spiritual and social past. The intangible elements exist today in a mélange of secular spirituality, e.g. competition seen as equivalent to honesty.

Secular spirituality is defined as: "the adherence to a spiritual philosophy without adherence to a religion" [5]. In *Management Mysterium*, secular spirituality means the human spirituality associated with material world. Despite the absence of a supernatural God and associated formal religion, classical economics, neoclassical economics, and neoliberalism are all part of a family of facts and faith that form a type of secular religion that is adhered to, more or less, by billions of people. It is easy to observe how economics has been influenced by theology. But the more important result is that, over time, economics has virtually become a theology, one in which "the markets" have taken on a secular religious and God-like significance in daily life. The market being the "ultimate concern," because it is believed to give meaning to everything else in life. It is the organizing principle, the secular spiritual center, of past and current times.

Much that pertains to Natural Rights, ownership, property, money, etc., is faith-based. The validity of many economic concepts is based more on faith – sometimes exclusively on faith. Discredited economic ideas live on: efficient market hypothesis, "trickle-down economics," privatization, austerity during economic expansions, and the end of economic volatility (Great Moderation). These and other zombie economic ideas are not evidence-based, and evidence against them won't kill them. The facts do not support the benefits or results that these ideas promote. Decades or centuries must pass to filter out worthless or time-worn ideas. Nevertheless, these and much older economic ideas are taken by many to be a permanent and useful part of the canon of the New Religion.

For the last 300-plus years, people of wealth and fame, and others less wealthy or notable, fully embrace the New Religion. And they vigorously defend it from encroachment – often in light of facts that undermine its foundational or later elements. This suggests a faith, or a secular spirituality, that is beyond reason. No value judgment is made here. Rather, it is important to recognize only that faith is integral to our understanding of economics and practice of economic transactions. Floating currency systems demand that we trust in God; the religious, agnostic, and atheist alike. There is no choice in the matter.

As one goes through their life, they think that the way things are today – how we think, understand, and do things generally, and especially in the management of business – is the good and efficient product of work that was done in the past using careful thought and analysis, facts and logic, and expert problem-solving honed through both experiments and trial-and-error. We disregard the possibility, indeed, the likelihood that there was little thought or analysis, avoidance of facts and the use of faulty logic, and that problem-solving was more a matter of expediency than understanding the causal sequence that generated the problem. Yet, the practice of management, both strategic and tactical, is mostly unscientific, and so management problems from 100 years ago remain with us today [6]. Therefore, our assumptions concerning how we think, understand, and do things in the management of organizations today must be grounded to some large degree in faith. That faith may be of a supernatural sort, but it is more likely secular.

Is this a problem? It is if the expectation and desire of individuals and society is for humans to make progress while time passes and as life changes. It is if people waste their precious lives and resources repeating errors because they have a bias against the past and prefer to ignore it. Secular spirituality can certainly be part of efforts to make progress, but it cannot be all of it because secular spirituality shines no light on causal sequence. To make progress, one must understand the sequence of cause and effect that occur when problems arise – management problems as well as technical problems, the latter being the usual domain for understanding causal sequence. However, there exists among most leaders an unsubstantiated belief that nothing better exists or can exist. Or, a denial that something better does exist. That no corporate management system is better than the current one – or society's social, economic, or political systems – so all that is necessary is to make some periodic minor adjustments to an otherwise sound system. Fundamentally, this view rests on a system of secular beliefs.

The next chapter will examine the secular spiritual beliefs of those who lead organizations, particularly business organizations, under the regime of classical management. The hope is to expand the reader's understanding of how and why secular spirituality exists, how it functions, and what it achieves. There is no desire on the part of the author to eliminate secular spirituality from leadership or business. That is both foolish and impossible to do. There is, however, a desire to learn and understand circumstances when secular spirituality leads to or contributes to results that are inconsistent with the strategy, goals, objectives articulated by business leaders or as desired by customers or society. This, in turn, can result in various types of failures, small or large, that negatively impact the corporation and its employees in various ways.

Hypocrisy notwithstanding, it seems that leaders have an earnest interest in personal and business success. Therefore, they might be open to learning more about how they think and make decisions. They may also be willing to learn more about business expertise – what is it, who has it, where is it in the organization, and how to make better use of it. Does all business expertise reside at the top of the company (see Note 4), or is it scattered throughout? And how can business expertise hidden in the organization be respected and brought forward? How can expertise be coordinated and used jointly rather than severally? Severally being the call during the Middle Ages. Is jointly the call of the Information Age and beyond? It might not seem like it, but maybe it is, once again.

Questions to Reflect On

- What Middle Age social values and sentiments have been carried over to today?
- What Middle Age economic ideas and values have been carried over to today?
- Do any Middle Age social or economic values make sense for today?
- In the Middle Ages, why did the conservative Church and State allow such major changes in power and property relations to take place? Could it happen again? How? See references [1] and [7] for ideas.
- What should society be in the 21st century: conservatively connected to tradition or progressive with timely change?
- Should the individual remain the focus of economic and social theory and practice? Or, is that less relevant today? Is there a better concept for humanity to flourish?
- How do you know when an idea, value, or sentiment is out of date and no longer useful? What would be the signs or evidence that it is no longer useful for current for future times? What or who would provide the evidence?
- Has "market economy" become an old idea? Will it someday be replaced by artificial intelligence as the means for making choices that humans once made? Will machine learning replace the "invisible hand?"

Notes

1. Property was originally conceived of as that which was produced by one's own (hand) labor using materials provided by nature and thus belongs to him, to use as he wishes. Today, the understanding of property is far removed from this early description.

2. Economic liberalism and current-day neoliberalism differ from the modern term "liberal" as used in a social or political context (i.e. electoral or liberal ideology).

3. As the centuries pass, individualism enters the personal realm and becomes the model for all human interests and activities, producing varied forms of detachment and de-socialization. Economic efficiency, as both means and ends, subverts the need for cooperation in complex integrated societies. The result is popularly known as "wealth inequality," but I think the more accurate term is "wealth unfairness" – the unwillingness to share wealth. In recent decades, labor productivity per hour increased at 2.5 times the rate of inflation adjusted wages (which have remained largely flat). Wealth creation is a social process, and therefore benefits must accrue to labor and to society, to aid the fulfillment of reciprocal social and moral commitments.

4. Leaders' interest in personal and business success is discolored by frequent failures. One such example, which commonly represents many others, is a gross misunderstanding (inability to learn) or willful ignorance (no interest in learning) of where expertise lies within an

organization, is how private equity bankrupted Payless ShoeSource. See Irwin, N. (2020), "How Private Equity Buries Payless," *The New York Times*, 31 January, https://nyti.ms/2S59Mlv

References

[1] Tawney, R.H. (1926), *Religion and the Rise of Capitalism: A Historical Study*, Harcourt, Brace and Company, Inc., New York, NY

[2] Friedman, B. M. (2011), "The Religious Roots of Modern Economics: Historical Origins and Contemporary Consequences," *Clemens Lecture Series No. 19*, St. John's University, https://digitalcommons.csbsju.edu/clemens_lectures/19

[3] Friedman, B. M. (2011), "Economics: A Moral Inquiry with Religious Origins," *American Economic Review: Papers & Proceedings*, Vol. 101, No. 3, 166–170, http://www.aeaweb.org/articles.php?doi=10.1257/aer.101.3.166

[4] For example, see Wayland, F. (1885), *The Elements of Political Economy*, recast by A. Chapin, Sheldon and Company, New York, NY

[5] See "Secular Spirituality," https://en.wikipedia.org/wiki/Secular_spirituality

[6] Emiliani, B. (2018), *The Triumph of Classical Management Over Lean Management: How Tradition Prevails and What to Do About It*, Cubic, LLC, South Kingstown, Rhode Island

[7] Heller, H. (2011), *The Birth of Capitalism: A Twenty-First-Century Perspective*, Pluto Press, London, U.K.

2
Classical Management Spirituality

"...the individual habitually applies the animistic or anthropomorphic formula in dealing with the facts of his environment. The animistic habit acts in all cases to blur the appreciation of causal sequence; but the earlier, less reflected, less defined animistic sense of propensity may be expected to affect the intellectual processes of the individual in a more pervasive way than the higher forms of anthropomorphism."

– Thorstein Veblen

Classical Management Spirituality

In feudal times, warfare was the most honorable of employments. The honor associated with warfare and fighting battles remains present in its full force today, but not just in the context of military action. It also applies to business affairs (see Note 1). "Business is war," as the saying goes. Top leaders, engaged in a pecuniary occupation (money and ownership), implicitly or explicitly see business as "war" because it is competitive ("us vs. them"), as is sports, and both are specialized forms of conflict. Business is competitive even if monopoly conditions exist because top management will work vigorously to exclude new entrants into the market. Much like a professional athlete whose competition has been lapped, the runner will continue the race as if competitors are close on one's heels.

Business has much in common with sports in the sense that it is zero-sum, there being a clear requirement for a winner and a loser. Matters are judged from the viewpoint of competition (the fight), money (placing bets), and ownership (winning). The goal is to vanquish one's rivals, thoroughly if possible, for greater showmanship, glory, and honor; to enhance one's status in business through invidious comparison. This spirituality is deeply embedded in this militaristic, atavistic, preconception of winning. War, predation, and like forms of exploit are the logical consequence of a more determined application of individualism and fixation on gain. Taking this perspective, a business can be seen as perpetually at "war" for as long as it exists. The question is, how do leaders fight business "war"? What is the course of action?

The risks being great suggest that prudence is the preferred approach, using the basic thinking and knowledge of business and the assets at hand [1]. Competitors follow the same conservative plan using the conventions (thinking, knowledge, and assets; see Note 2) that have long existed – absent all skepticism. Leaders conspicuously emulate the thinking and actions of other leaders, which confers respect to them in an obvious devotional or ceremonial manner. When a person of high status, the CEO, solves a business problem in a certain way, other leaders uncritically accept that solution as gospel because of who the leader is, not because the CEO presented any understanding of the causal sequence (the facts) that led to the problem.

Consequently, there is a spiritual belief that CEOs can successfully dictate a course of action (direct resources) without knowing the ground-level facts of the situation, and a mystical union between distant leaders that automatically compels them to copy one another. For example, a former CEO of General Electric thought it more wise to subject employees to forced rankings than understand the root causes of unsatisfactory performance. Other CEOs, witnessing this bold method of competitive ranking for lower-status employees, happily followed along believing that they too would benefit from the showmanship, glory, and honor that accompanies barbarous action.

Conflict being the normal course of business meant that leaders should celebrate the internal strife among lower-status employees that was created by the forced rankings. Years passed before forced rankings were discredited, and still more years passed before business leaders would come to realize the destruction caused by forced rankings. Nevertheless, it is likely that a prominent CEO will someday praise and authorize forced rankings, giving license for many other leaders to follow. The lessons of the past will be lost, as they usually are, because, in business, as in other affairs, the past never seems relevant to those presently in power. This view, again, is of a spiritual nature whereby leaders are somehow supernaturally endowed with all the knowledge and wisdom necessary to succeed in the present and magically inoculated against all failures of past leaders.

Business, like sport, is deeply imbued with secular spirituality: superstitions, belief in luck (betting), magic, mysticism, and mythology. The supernatural is commonly believed to be a contributing factor in one's success in competitive rankings, either as individuals (wealth, status, and privilege) or as business enterprise (sales, profits, number of employees). The Divine Right of Kings and Queens (Figure 2-1) has its secular materialistic analog, which is the right to corporate leadership granted by the gods of vainglorious competition.

Having won such favor, it is vulgar for those of inferior status to cast doubt upon the leader. Mystically, the leader's decisions cannot be challenged or questioned – at least not easily challenged or questioned. Public dressing-down of those who question the boss casts a lasting pall (spell) over everyone. Companies are closer in structure to feudal society than one might care to admit, possessing a precisely ordered and graded hierarchy of status and functions. Who has not heard their boss say: "Do it because I told you so," or some variant thereof, explicitly or implicitly? Employees are compelled to give their consent for leaders to do as they please, believing that what is good for the leader or good for the company is good for them as well. The hierarchy of authoritarian control assures compliance, not curiosity, not creativity, and status quo, not progress.

Descended from divine right, secular leaders feel no obligation to understand the facts or bargain with those who do. In one organization after another, this is not recognized as a disease transmitted from the top leader to all leaders below. The disease is rarely contained and thus

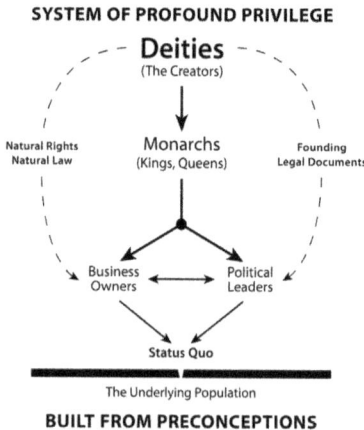

Figure 2-1. In the System of Profound Privilege (SoPP), leaders are descended from deities, and their thinking and decisions are built from preconceptions which function as a type of spiritual discipline.

delays the timely emergence of the new and better.

There is also a mystical relationship among the members, past and present, of the society of CEOs in which the sanctity of one's opinions, judgments, and actions are determined by how large a company is in terms of its annual sales. Figure 2-2 shows the hierarchy of CEO gods, wherein minor CEO gods lead companies whose sales are in the millions, and major CEO gods lead companies whose sales are in the billions. The minor CEO gods are influenced by those nearest to them in the hierarchy, and so on up the line until one gets to the top CEO god whose word is the most sacred and venerated of all. It is through this process of leadership mystification that causal sequence, the facts as they exist at lower levels, become less and less relevant to business administration. As a result, the pace of change lags far behind that needed to keep up with the times.

For at least the last 50 years, human interests, needs, and desires have been changing at a rate faster than existing systems. This is self-evident (see Note 3). Established long ago, these systems are operated by leaders with an eye single to preserving the status quo. Eventually, this will lead to historically significant social disruption. It is therefore useful to understand the many variables that are in play – economic, social, political, historical, philosophical, legal, business, and spiritual – when substantial change is sought by people, whether that comprises employees in a company or society at-large. Changes must be made to all, or occur in all, of the eight variables, and business leaders in the highest levels of the social hierarchy are faced with the decision to

Hierarchy of
CEO Gods

$500 Billion	**Major God**
$100 Billion	
$10 Billion	
$1 Billion	
$100 Million	
$10 Million	
$1 Million	Minor God

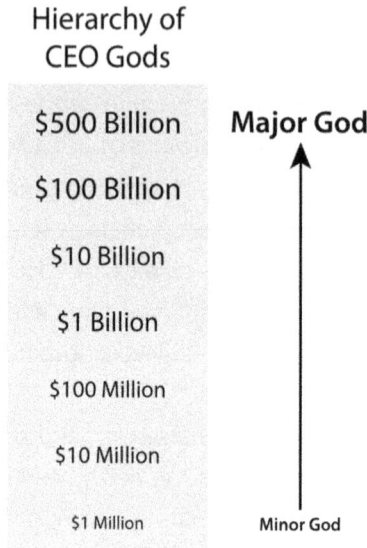

Figure 2-2. Hierarchy of CEO gods in terms of annual sales.

resist, allow, or personally engage in producing the needed changes.

The numerous (10-20 or more) preconceptions associated with each of the eight variables – economic, social, political, historical, philosophical, legal, business, and spiritual – help enshrine the status quo so that any problem in business, leadership, or management can be traced back to them. A common problem-solving method for determining root causes is the Ishikawa (fishbone) diagram. It graphically illustrates the relationship between a problem (the effect) and the six cause categories: materials, methods, machine, measurement, worker, and environment. A parallel construction expressing cause and effect can be made, as shown in Figure 2-3. The "preconception diagram" can be

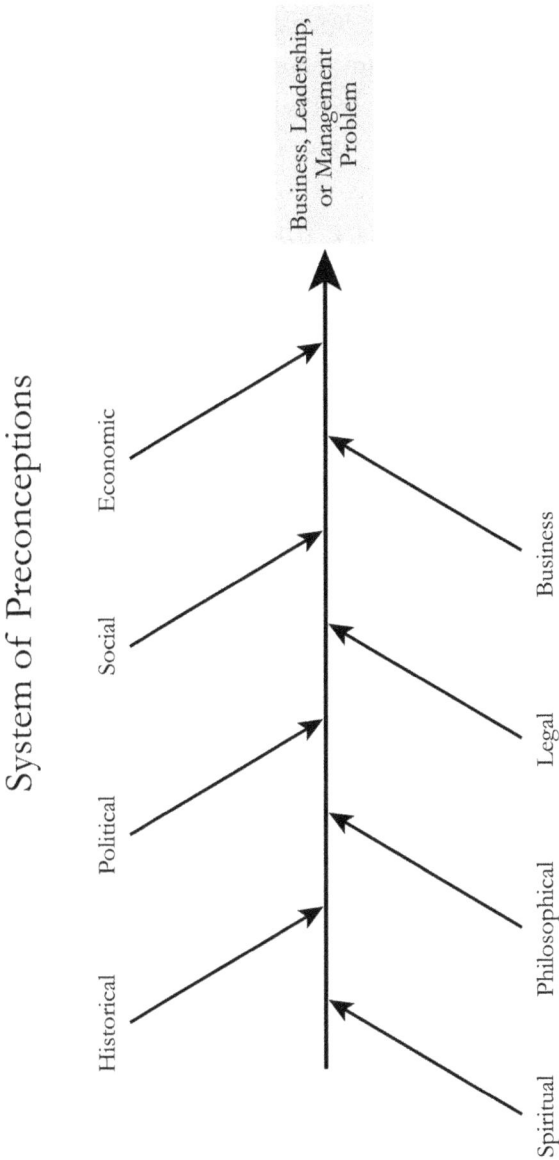

Figure 2-3. Preconception diagram to identify the root cause of business, leadership, or management problems. Try it out.

used to identify the management preconceptions that produced the problem. Subsequent action would be to eliminate manager's preconceptions to avoid recurrence of the problem. Diligent use of this method by leaders will reveal recurring patterns of thinking that persistently downgrade organizational efficiency and effectiveness. Yet, the type of work one does or does not do depends upon one's status.

Top leaders do not engage in structured problem-solving methods. Their usual method of problem-solving is analysis of data provided to them, conversation, deliberation, and directive consistent with conservative plans and past conventions, as these have been accredited by generations of leaders engaged in an occupation whose narrow focus is money and ownership. Alternatively, they may ask a peer CEO what to do. Either way, the problem-solving process lacks rigor and connection to ground-level facts. Leaders view the use of structured problem-solving methods as the province of the lowest levels of the organization, to ensure that their work continues apace and to avoid disturbing top leaders from their pecuniary pursuits. Only workers' problem-solving processes require rigor and connection to the facts.

The low-level workers who deal with facts are persistently at a disadvantage when they seek needed change from their superiors. The facts are no match for the spiritual and tradition-laden rhetoric employed by leaders. It is more convincing, and it discourages initiative. Persuasive arguments, incorporating faith more than facts, can be made that the current system is fundamentally sound and workable, meaning, it is efficient or good enough to provide the needed results. Humans, as spiritual creatures, are subject to easy manipulation, and readily sacrifice themselves for the interests of the company. We want to believe our leaders and give them the benefit of any doubts. Their "gut" response to problems is good enough.

In contrast, Lean management is seen as a high ideal, not as a workable system that produces useful benefits. What leaders really mean is that eliminating waste destroys vested interests, a supremely unappealing proposition for them, but not so for society. There is a deep spirituality associated with pragmatism, which in business invariably means expediency. Leaders have no time or desire to turn all problems, especially *their* problems, over to scientific thinking. To do so would violate the fundamental belief in the universal applicability and effectiveness of conservative plans, past conventions, and expediency, and thus undercut leaders' prerogatives – their rights and privileges.

Instead, what top business leaders want from followers is loyalty, whether their directives are genius or disastrous, and whether they are models of good behavior or criminals. Loyalty, therefore, is a quality that is of the spiritual, mystical, or occult realm. Loyal followers must possess some belief in the secular divine existence and capabilities of their leader, and that their interests magically coincide with those of top leaders. Their followership is defined by an acceptance of dependent thinking and manipulation for ends that may be contrary to their own interests. This is a form of ceremonial behavior implanted through socialization to imbue respect for convention and authority, status, prestige, privileges. It is legitimized through tradition and absorbs others lower in the hierarchy into this adhesive relationship that is certain to one day be problematic for all.

The need for loyalty, part of the spiritual realm associated with war (competition) and predation (grinding down the poor), disables top leaders' ability to be curious and develop the peaceful skills of workmanship (i.e. craftsmanship) that are needed to deftly lead organizations as times change. Leaders' preservation and maintenance of the status quo is thus a result of both clear-minded intentionality as well as the unwitting embrace of customs common to leadership and the preservation of one's status and privileges.

Loyalty, which engenders arbitrary and absolute exercise of authority to perpetuate the status quo, is not limited to interpersonal relationships. It extends to systems, such as the corporate management system and its economic, social, and political relations. Leaders have great loyalty towards the New Religion: economic liberalism; the market-based economic system, its defining features of economic liberalism and associated mysticism and spiritual beliefs (invisible hand, *laissez faire*, "tax cuts pay for themselves"), and its sacred system of power and property relations (see Note 4). These generate unshakable preconceptions (e.g. the market or tax code is the solution to every economic, social or political problem; private enterprise can do anything better than government), that results in great and long-lasting conflicts between people with different learned views or those who recognize when centuries-old ideas – in whole or part – are no longer useful or must be adjusted to reflect current times (see Note 5). Adhering to the past is a spiritual embrace that does not reflect the facts of current times and the improvements that need to be made.

For leaders, the preservation of long-established preconceptions and systems are well worth fighting for. It is popularly said that "facts are inconvenient." But they are much more than just inconvenient. Facts undermine the effectiveness of the spiritual, mystical, and occult aspects of leadership. Conversely, the spiritual, mystical, and occult aspects of leadership can easily crush the facts. The spiritual, mystical, and occult aspects of leadership are value-laden, while scientific thinking must be objective and value-free. It is difficult to think of a more consequential disunion in human affairs than this. One seeks to obfuscate and suppress progress, while the other seeks to discover the truth and enable progress. The former has continuous power, the latter has only intermittent power – on the much longer time scale of centuries. While there is an appearance of progress, society (at-large or the microcosm of the corporation) is, in fact, falling into arrears. The spiritual, mystical, occult, and atavistic aspects of leadership make incremental deterioration more likely than incremental improvement. But people are too easily persuaded by sophistic arguments that it is otherwise, given their many vulnerabilities and attachments in life (see Note 6).

The faithful and boundless success orientation of business leaders brings this to fruition. The cocksure certainty that anything the top leader says or does is preordained for success is a superstition that generates a false view of reality and an idolic sense of one's self. Competence, curiosity, and concern for others are retrograde to this superstition. They are seen as either so common as to be of minor interest or unnecessary to the well-being of the corporate body and its internal and external dependents. Status brings one nearer to royalty which brings one nearer to God, which satisfies an outsized desire for worth and meaning, and the avoidance of futility in one's life. To be someone important, to have power, to be able to tell people what to do, is to feel like or be like a god. But in whose service; self or others?

When problems arise, leaders invariably blame others – usually, "a few bad apples." Both leaders and followers accept this explanation: leaders because they cannot believe they are poor or incompetent at doing their job, and followers because they want to trust their leaders and have faith in them that they are capable and in control of the organization. The mythologizing of top leaders leads to an inverse relationship between authority and competency. Leaders want to believe, in some occult way, that problems are always caused by workers somewhere in the bottom half of the organization and that problems are limited in scope. In the absence of scientific thinking, there is only a spiritual path for correcting problems in simplistic ways. Superstitions reduce the effectiveness of management's work which impairs the organization and its ability to respond to changing conditions.

Organizations are destined for conflict between leaders and workers due to differences in beliefs, inclusive of the forms of secular spirituality that exist in each working realm. Problems, conflicts, status differences, etc., lead top managers to take on a dislike for workers and so they seek to eliminate human labor where possible. But the root of the problem is in the direction of a conflict between leaders' preconceptions and workers' perceptions, as shown in Figure 2-3. Leaders and workers both believe in the truth of what they know and do, yet the uneven power relationship virtually assures that leaders' time-traveled preconceptions overrule workers' up-to-the-minute sensory perceptions.

Belief Spectrum

Preconceptions	Perceptions
Learn-by-Talking	Learn-by-Doing
Listening	Seeing
Opinions	Facts
Books	Know-How

Figure 2-3. Leaders, guided mostly by preconceptions, are far removed from the sensory perceptions that guide workers in their work. Leaders, who were at one time workers, drift from right to left as they are promoted. The sweet spot for leaders is to the right of center.

The chasm between leaders' aged and inaccurate preconceptions and workers current and accurate perceptions is how businesses get into big trouble and how everyone is made to suffer. All one need do is think of Autostrade and the Morandi bridge collapse, Boeing and the 737 Max crashes, BP and the Gulf of Mexico oil spill, drug makers and distributors and the opioid epidemic, General Electric and failed financial engineering, General Motors and the fatal ignition switch, U.K. social housing and the deadly Grenfell Tower fire, Vale and the mining dam disaster, Wells Fargo and consumer fraud, and the list goes on and on. Yet, the faithful and boundless success orientation of business leaders blinds them to these failures and their valuable lessons due to leaders' faulty preconceptions and ignorance of workers' accurate sensory perceptions. Corporate cultures, a reflection of leaders' preconceptions and secular spiritualty, subordinate the perceptions and spirituality that exists at the working-level which continuously and selflessly warns of current or future danger. The mythology of leadership and corporate preeminence and the mystification of failure (i.e. "a few bad apples," "we adhere to the highest standards") serves no one, not even leaders. It merely perpetuates primitive, atavistic thinking.

Recall that in the Middle Ages, neither the Church nor the State viewed the feudal system as having anything to do with poverty. It was instead due to the personal demerit of the poor and needy. For business leaders, it is likewise inconceivable that the leader's preconceptions, management system, or business processes that they are responsible for could be the cause of poor organizational performance. Instead, it is the fault of the workers, proof of their inabilities. Whether you get good guidance from your boss, or not, you are personally and individually responsible for the results, even under conditions of teamwork. It's your success, or your fault, alone. This, again, is condemnation whose origin is spiritual, not factual. Similarly, there is a superstition among leaders that they possess superior abilities in all its manifest forms. This results in an inability common among leaders to recognize their own lack of ability, which suggests a deep spiritual basis for the Dunning-Kruger effect [2]. Meaning, leaders cannot comprehend the possibility that they lack competence.

This brings us to the heart of the matter. We have seen many ways in which leaders' thinking and actions are informed by the sanctity of Natural Rights, economic liberalism, property rights, money, freedom, competition, and so on, and the secular spirituality, supernatural, occult, mysticism, and mythology associated with these. This affects how leaders construct reality, perceive problems, process information, and how they interpret and respond to business problems. The created reality has greater authenticity and validity than ground-level phenomena and cause and effect. The result is simplistic solutions to business problems, and thus to keep in abeyance the systems, methods, tools that have been proven to result in improvement.

Generally, any major business problem is construed as some form of financial problem. To CEOs, almost any financial problem is corrected by three simplistic solutions: lay people off, close facilities, and squeeze suppliers for lower prices (see Note 7). This common course of action, centuries-old, reveals a complete disinterest in causality – causal sequence or cause and effect. Secular spirituality is non-causal; it is not the domain of cause and effect. It offers no causal explanation for existential business phenomena – namely, financial or other types of problems. Leaders exempt themselves from having to think in terms of causality, as priests do (but for different reasons). It is not their traditional intellectual domain. Facts, such as they are delivered to leaders by subordinates, come distorted or are discounted by leaders to grant conformance to their reality as colored by the spiritual demands of status, honor, and privilege. Hence the use of the same simplistic solutions to recurring (or any) business problems – lay people off, close facilities, and squeeze suppliers. One might guess, correctly, leaders who are better attuned to ground-level cause and effect largely avoid such problems to begin with. The facts are gospel, not the leaders' word. Yet no one is shocked to learn that tardily reacting to problems confers valuable heroic and honorific credentials, while problem avoidance does not, and so the former is a better and more trustworthy measure of one's status and capabilities.

When new facts and data are presented, leaders' reasoning is invariably through the lens of convention – the thinking and actions common to other leaders (money, ownership, competition, freedom) – rather than a revision of one's understanding of the problem which, in turn, would suggest actions inconsistent with the usual conventions. Therefore, facts are made to conform with existing knowledge and preconceptions, rather than changing one's knowledge and preconceptions to conform to the facts of the matter. The former leads to the simplistic, atavistic solutions of belittling, criticizing, threatening, or blaming people. In such situations, it is clear that causality is spiritually imputed, in the required unsophisticated yet authoritative way, to one or more delinquent employees somewhere down the hierarchy. The end or final cause of a problem is people judged by the leader to have not done their job correctly. Leaders' predominant theory of business problems is people failing (anthropomorphizing problems), as shown in Figure 2-4, not poor leadership, not poor day-to-day management, not poor policies, not poor business processes, and not poor metrics.

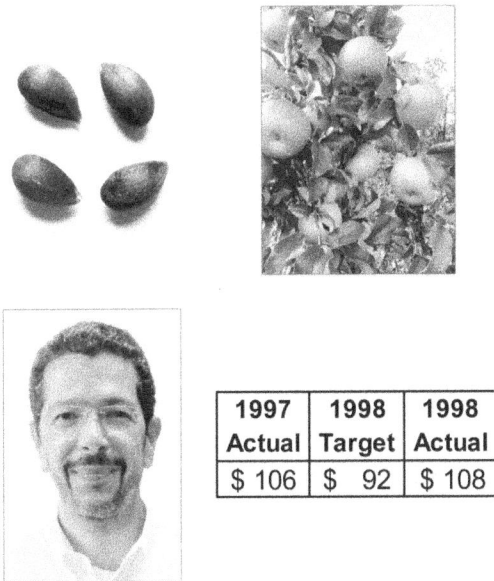

1997	1998	1998
Actual	Target	Actual
$ 106	$ 92	$ 108

Figure 2-4. Just as apple seeds grow and produce apple trees, people fail and produce problems.

The inability of leaders to move beyond a primitive understanding of causality, blaming people for problems – the universal explanation – traces back to their divine right

(Figure 2-1). In addition, the spiritual structure of leadership penetrates all thought on matters economic, social, political, historical, philosophical, legal, and business, and is fixed into place by scores of aged preconceptions. When leaders think uncritically, opinions become normalized as valid substitutes for facts, which other people then copy as if leaders' opinions are facts. Under such conditions, business expertise is a façade that easily fools people. The actual business expertise that exists in the organization goes unrecognized or underground seeking safety.

It seems that the failure to understand the true relationships between the causes that produce an effect (problem) lies solely with leaders. It is their personal failing. There is some truth to this in the sense that most leaders see problems as bad; things that are dirty or impure, a foul-smell rising from the sweaty bottom of the organization that causes them great discomfort. The much larger fault lies with the fundamental design characteristics and traditions of leadership, which condemns leaders to spiritually imputed, atavistic management thinking and actions that cannot be stated in terms of cause and effect. Perhaps too, the habit of mind that causes leaders to imagine problems in personal terms, as an affront to their status and well-being, also lies with the basic design and traditions of leadership. But that can be corrected if there is the will to do it.

Understanding causal sequence requires leaders to understand systems in ways far better than faith or mere theoretical conceptualizations coupled with preconceptions that further degrade comprehension. Yet workmanship to leaders means to "make the numbers" – to understand levers, not to understand systems – and the secular spirituality that guides leaders' thinking and actions is ultimately reducible to non-productive salesmanship (bullshit) that inhibits employees' workmanship. The propensity of leaders for widespread uncritical acceptance of a range of matters related to business leaves them, the company, customers, and others vulnerable to disasters. For example, under the regime of classical management, the management, system, policies, and processes are more or less uncritically accepted by the current top leader as well as their predecessors and successors. Metrics and KPIs (key performance indicators) are a particularly noteworthy example. The large suite of metaphysical corporate metrics is uncritically questioned by leaders and believed to be, in some occult way, both right and good, and pursued with near-religious fervor. It is further believed that people are managing to the metric – and those who miss the numbers have sinned and are required by corporate scripture to explain variances in Confession (management reviews). This is a fantasy that helps explain why actual improvement of systems and processes is so elusive (see Note 8).

Sales and other types of business forecast, the spiritual belief in the ability to predict the future, is another example of how spirituality commands leaders and others to labor under hoped-for realities. Corporate politics are another form of spirituality, coupled with ceremonialism, in which the illusion of favorable appearances is of higher authenticity and more valid than the facts pertaining to the existence of widespread organizational dysfunction. Vision, strategy, synergy, teamwork, etc., are fundamentally spiritual and mystical in nature. For leaders, the spiritual and mystical are easier for them to engage, both mentally and physically, than to deal with the facts of the matter as produced by ground-level cause and effect. Uncritical examination of the long spiritual and mystical traditions associated with leadership makes it seem as if these are still relevant today, in full force. But they are not. The need for today is understanding systems and causality, not continuing along in the leisurely tasks of fortune-telling and giving orders. The need is to disqualify simplistic solutions, despite leaders' right to them.

Spirituality and mysticism exist with respect to the efficacy of meetings: team meetings, department meetings, all-hands meetings, skip-level meetings, executive retreats, and so on. These ceremonial forms of information-sharing are believed by managers to be of value. To believe that, they must substantially discount the existence of, or trouble which may be caused by, power relationships, department or individual rivalries, passive-aggressive behaviors, disinterest, and apathy. Most meetings are run in ways that reflect past conventions, a form of dissipation that fit managers' preferred scheme of value in organizations. Meetings between lower-level employees and senior managers are notable for the lack of notetaking by managers, suggesting that problems identified by workers are not the subject of senior managers' interests.

This reflects a *laissez faire* attitude about ground-level problems and that management engagement with employees is a façade; that showmanship and a gambling spirit matters far more than competence. Other ceremonial observances include deal making (mergers, acquisitions and divestitures, i.e. gambling, which invokes the need for luck), presentations, business unit reviews, celebrations for success, requiems for layoffs, investor roadshows, webcasts and conference calls. These sacraments strengthen spiritual attachment and corporate mysticism.

Within the executive ranks and executive teams generally, "good chemistry" between people is a desirable and sought-after quality that rests on grounds of superstition. Top leaders claim that mergers and acquisitions (trophies) will result in "synergies," which also rests on grounds of superstition. The notion of "teamwork" resides in leaders' minds as a theoretical, idealized conception of lower-level people working closely together in the absence of any forms of struggle, conflict, or imperfection. This too rests on grounds of superstition. Likewise, the idea that people are doing their job function as leaders imagine them to be doing. It is magical thinking by leaders to believe that these desirable conditions happen automatically under the aegis of classical management wherein people are more concerned about themselves than they are about others.

Diversity also exists on the grounds of a superstition in which women, people of color, and people with different sexual orientations are hired for better representation in thinking and decision-making. Yet, a common experience among the diverse is continued exclusion under the banner of inclusion. Their presence may be valued in terms of appearance, a metric, or other score, but their contributions in the form of thinking differently are not. Traditional modes of thinking and doing, reflective of top leadership, means diverse viewpoints coming from people who look different are often not listened to, particularly when it comes to making important decisions. Diversity is more decorous or symbolic, rather than seen by leaders as producing a material advantage towards improved business efficiency and greater success. The ceremonial text (playbook) for success in business was established long ago, and diversity remains absent [1]. As such, diversity, as it is presently practiced, occupies the spiritual realm.

As this chapter has endeavored to reveal, in the context of business, human intelligence normally rises only to the level of average: an intelligence quotient (IQ) of 90 to 109. This will no doubt offend the tender sensibilities of top leaders, but the case has been made that a spiritual habit of mind, coupled with disregard for ground-level cause and effect, greatly dulls one's intelligence. Management's function is not to create a world, systems and processes, of make-believe, it is to understand the systems and processes as they are and lead accordingly.

To the extent that one believes in emotional intelligence (EQ), one can say that under classical management that EQ is as low or lower than IQ. The Divine Right of Kings and Queens deeply believe it necessary for their inferiors to work in a constant state of fear, mostly to perpetuate their grasp on people and to retain their rights and privileges. In this context, psychological safety is irrelevant. Providing it to employees is impossible because psychological safety results in economic, social, political, and philosophical costs that leaders do not want to incur (see Note 9). Under the regime of classical management, fear is useful to leaders. It quickly conditions employees to fit in and do what the boss says. Employees must display loyalty and subordination to their superiors and commit themselves to rapid response to problems or unfavorable metrics, such that their correction benefits the leader. It does not matter if the problem is big or small, infrequent or a daily occurrence. What matters is that workers respond quickly and that they effectively ameliorate the problem by any means. Psychological danger keeps employees on a war-like footing where even small problems are to be treated as emergencies. Relatedly, hierarchies are seen by leaders as having benefits in terms of order and control. It is easy to understand and serviceable despite any shortcomings. One only needs to ask: "What does the boss want?"

It should not be surprising that classically managed organizations have numerous chronic ailments. Employees don't understand the strategy, communication is poor, departments work at odds with one another, products and services have quality problems, deliveries perpetually late, key initiatives run behind schedule and over budget, and so on. Leaders are not completely unaware or complacent. They sometimes recognize these chronic problems and seek solutions (an honorific act), often with the help of consultants who are loath to criticize them for their poor leadership which everyone can easily see. Instead, they discuss the narrow range of available options and agree on ameliorative measures – typically, the latest management fad – commonly known as being wasteful. But a management fad is useful for keeping up appearance and avoid having to set the pace. It is the standard solution to business problems because most leaders cannot and will not seek to understand the root cause(s) of problems. Nor will consultants. Doing so would expose vast, glaring, and embarrassing ineptitude. Leaders cannot be blamed, though on rare occasions that steadfast rule is accidentally broken (see Note 10).

To avoid exposing deficiency, the spiritual is deftly employed in pursuit of the material. More importantly, the spiritual is inseparable from the material (Figure 2-5); the former is required in order to obtain the latter. The spiritual mobilizes employees to preserve and expand the company's interests and maintain its place of honor in society, aided by sacred objects such as financial statements, patents, trademarks, and the heroic go-getters who consistently

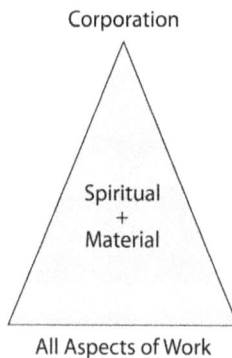

Corporation

Spiritual
+
Material

All Aspects of Work

Figure 2-5. The corporation is the ultimate authority over all aspects of work, combining the spiritual with the material to achieve desired business outcomes.

deliver results. In this way, the corporation is the ultimate authority over all aspects of work. Employees and other interested parties give consent to their betters to take as they please, under the superstition that leaders are of a higher order that can successfully traffic in the unknowable.

The manifold deficiencies, dysfunctionalities, and defects inherent to classical management in its usual practice by most leaders are the result of vigorous efforts to maintain the status quo. These efforts are both intentional as well as unintentional, but the former is in greatest effect. Leaders' have boundless faith in the traditions, preconceptions, and the efficacy of solutions to problems that precede one's time in the position of leader. Or, more importantly, the boundless faith in the falsity of all criticism of the traditions, preconceptions, and the efficacy of solutions to problems that precede one's time in the position of leader. These turn what should be a leader's greatest strength, to fluidly respond to problems as they emerge, into a monolith that erodes only slowly over time. The Divine Rights of the Kingdom (company) and the King and Queen (top leaders) are the most important thing. Causal sequence, reflection, and improvement are not. It is easy, reputable work at the top, but difficult and ignoble work for everyone else.

Given these facts, it is not difficult to see that the humanity of classical management, both spiritual and material, has been unsatisfactory for quite some time. The next chapter examines secular spirituality in Lean management and how is used to impart a positive human touch to the administration of business affairs. We learn how spirituality is used to enable progress instead of maintaining the status quo, and how it prepares people at all levels to be flexible and responsive to changing conditions.

Questions to Reflect On

- In business, where or when is uncritical acceptance appropriate or necessary and where or when is it not?
- Can you identify secular spiritual beliefs that improve the efficiency of your work, your department, or your company? Are there any that impair work?
- Can you identify evidence-based facts that improve the efficiency of your work, your department, or your company? Are there any that impair work?
- Why does classical management have little or no regard for understanding the causal sequence of problems? List 10 reasons. Identify the root cause(s).
- What types or forms of secular spirituality undermine discovery of causal sequence and the facts of a problem?
- Generations of managers since the late 1800s have faced the same or similar types of business problems, from supervisor to CEO. To each generation, the problems are new to them. What spiritual beliefs account for this view among the those who are entrusted with the lives and livelihoods of others?
- Oddly, business being a hostile, competitive environment produces much low-effort thinking (heuristics) by managers at all levels. Given that leadership begins at the top, what can be done to produce more high-effort (causal) thinking?
- Buzzwords are part of the arcana of classical management. Which buzzwords reflect spiritual beliefs?

Notes

1. Predatory behavior has long been recognized as honorific, whether it is killing the beast, fighting in battle, or the hostile (or friendly) takeover of a competing company. In business as elsewhere, persons (mainly men) are selected for duty based on their spiritual fitness for the malevolent work of predation and trained accordingly. It should be noted that the prospect of future financial gains is sold to investors based on earnest faith and glossy promotion. Predation is ever-present within this realm, and the CEO is chieftain of business combat.

2. The basic thinking and knowledge of business and the assets at hand come under the general headings of "business principles" and "business logic" (together, "business values"). These are the pecuniary principles and pecuniary logic associated with ownership (property rights) and the freedom to pursue self-interest (gain); i.e. to do what is most advantageous towards the achievement of one's ends.

3. Much as the underlying population in the Middle Ages grew tired of repressive feudalism and sought change, the younger generations of employees today are dissatisfied with corporate feudalism and the status quo. While they are mostly aligned with the corporation's interests, they seek greater involvement in decision-making, freedom to question superiors, freedom to try new ideas, and freedom to demand that corporate economic activity reduces various forms of externalized harms to society and the planet. Subservience and complying with authority (agreeing with

the boss) have their limits. Abnegation of one's own thinking and the facts violates what it means to be human. However, as entrepreneurial organizations grow in size and scale (e.g. Google), top leaders exert their power and authority to gain greater control over independent-minded employees by imposing new policies and rules. This short-term fix will, in the long run, likely fall short. The future of corporate governance may include new forms of worker representation to broaden management's interests beyond competitive gain, and to modify and update the spiritual constitution and temperament of senior leaders.

4. Mainstream (neoclassical) economists, followed by politicians and business leaders, have been the producer and directors of the New Religion. They are secular versions of Pope, Cardinals, and Archbishops. In this scheme of understanding, Bishops, Priests, and Deacons would be vice presidents, general managers, and middle managers. Together, over several decades, they have successfully advanced a system that has produced bimodal economic, social, and political outcomes, and a diminution of democratic ideals. Conserving classical management can be seen as an implicit defense of (globally accepted) Western ideas and way of life, regardless of outcomes.

5. For example, the 17th century understanding of "individualism" made sense in the feudal era, when handicraft and trade was conducted on a small, mostly individual scale (e.g. blacksmith, butcher, weaver, farmer). But post-Industrial Revolution, the scale of business changed and so did people's work. Machine processes

and division of labor should have us re-examine the merits of economic individualism in post-modern times. In doing so, the understanding of "individualism" would be updated replaced with "teamwork," which typically means people working together in teams of two to 12 or 15 people, reflecting needed social ties. Such a change might be effective at amelioration the self-interested behaviors associated with maximizing one's gains in economic transaction and produce benefits to society. Another thing to objectively examine, free of economic, political, or social ideology, is where markets work well and where they do not work so well in relation to the public (team society) interest and make adjustments accordingly. Systems (management systems and markets) must be responsive to human life, with efficiency being a secondary consideration.

6. The spiritual rhetoric of classical management is also helpful for identifying true believers and weeding out those who are less enthusiastic. The former are candidates for promotion, thus preserving unity in the leadership ranks and, consequently, in the levels below.

7. The triad of simplistic solutions, lay people off, close facilities, and squeeze suppliers for lower prices, are akin to an ancient religious ritual applied to business. That is, to sacrifice the weak in order to save the strong, where the strong is the corporate body and its leaders.

8. See "Metrics Madness. 'What Gets Measured Gets Managed?' Examining the Gaps Between Manager's Beliefs About Metrics and What Workers Actually Do," by Bob

Emiliani, 29 July 2017, https://bobemiliani.com/goodies/ Metrics-BBCs.pdf. Leaders operate under the illusion that if the metric is good, the decisions based on the metric are good, and the results of the decision will be good. Additionally, leaders are indifferent to critically examining metrics because even bad metrics serve a useful function: the exercise of power and compliance. That is, to keep employees in a perpetual state of high alert, ready to spring into action to ameliorate an unfavorable number, in the mystical belief that this is good business practice. To understand the flaws in this argument, see Graban, M. (2019), *Measures of Success: React Less. Lead Better. Improve More*, Constancy, Inc., Colleyville, Texas. https://www. amazon.com/Measures-Success-React-Better-Improve/dp/ 1733519416/

9. Providing psychological safety to workers presumes that they are willing to alter their social networks, which can appear to them as a loss much larger than any gain. Efforts by the Lean community to show top leaders that it is safe to adopt Lean management usually fail because leaders are more concerned about avoiding present losses than they are about future gains from Lean. See Introduction, Note 4.

10. Among top leaders, hypocrisy is *de rigueur*, but publicly speaking ill of one's brethren, whether it is true or not, is taboo; it is a breach of faith and cultish devotion. In a profoundly discourteous and dishonorable act unbefitting a former CEO, Boeing's new CEO, David Calhoun, a member of Boeing's board of directors since 2009, blamed the past CEO, Dennis Muilenburg, for Boeing's vast

problems. See Kitroeff, N. and Gelles, D. (2020), "'It's More Than I Imagined': Boeing's New C.E.O. Confronts Its Challenges," *The New York Times*, 5 March, https://nyti.ms/2wwwUCi. Upon realizing his unseemly transgression of executive decorum, Calhoun apologized the next day. See Snider, A. and Tangel, A. (2020), "Boeing CEO Dave Calhoun Expresses Regret Over Criticisms of Leadership and Predecessor," *The Wall Street Journal*, 7 March, https://www.wsj.com/articles/boeing-ceo-dave-calhoun-expresses-regret-over-criticisms-of-leadership-and-predecessor-11583619577.

References

[1] Emiliani, B. (2018), *The Triumph of Classical Management Over Lean Management: How Tradition Prevails and What to Do About It*, Cubic, LLC, South Kingstown, Rhode Island, page 34, Table 1-2, "CEOs Wealth Creation Playbook."

[2] Kruger, J. and Dunning, D. (1999), "Unskilled and Unaware of It: How Difficulties in Recognizing One's Own Incompetence Lead to Inflated Self-Assessments," *Journal of Personality and Social Psychology*. Vol. 77, No. 6, pp. 1121-1134

3
Lean Management
Spirituality

"[The] animistic explanation of phenomena is a form of the fallacy which the logicians knew by the name of *ignava ratio*. For the purposes of industry or of science it counts as a blunder in the apprehension and valuation of facts."

– Thorstein Veblen

Lean Management and Spirituality

As Chapters 2 and 3 have shown, the material and spiritual grounds for classical management thinking and practice were laid down centuries ago. In the intervening years, practical changes were made to the economic, social, political, historical, philosophical, legal, and business grounds that strengthened its foundation. What we experience today has yet to be the apex of this line of thinking, as further strengthening is likely. But if it somehow changes course, it might re-emerge in the future after a short interruption. The material and spiritual grounds of classical management thinking and practice are strong and devoutly worshipped by many people holding high positions in society.

No similar material and spiritual grounds have been laid down across all of society for Toyota's (or Lean) management thinking and practice. That is a great limitation, but it does not spell doom. Toyota's management system (TMS) was developed to a large degree within the existing framework of the New Religion. The first president of Toyota Motor Corporation, Kiichiro Toyoda, had this to say about business and economics in the fall of 1945, eight years after the company was founded [1] (see Note 1):

> "We have finally come to the point where Japan will have to convert to a free market economy like that of the United States and compete with the rest of the world on an equal basis. We must therefore reform our protected and monopolistic companies.

The Japanese auto industry has been fostered and protected in a controlled economy and has never braved the rough waves of a free market situation... Moreover, viewed impartially from a global standpoint, Toyota is far from being a first-class company... we should see ourselves as something like a third-class auto company.

We will find it difficult to hold a clear course without foundering in the stormy seas of a free market economy. The ability of this company, which has sustained heavy blows, to make the transition from a controlled to a free market economy will determine its ultimate success or failure. However, if we can succeed in a free market economy, we will have a bright future ahead of us. Everything depends upon our own determination."

Toyota's management system, and its derivative Lean management, both being adaptable, can survive long-term on the antiquated grounds of the New Religion. But it can do so successfully only under a different type of leadership. The specific type of leadership is one who is not bound by all the available economic, social, political, historical, philosophical, legal, and business preconceptions. Generally, to become an effective Lean leader, to break the status quo, is a simultaneous process of unlearning and learning. The ever-present danger to this innovative management system is changes in leadership or changes in ownership which usually precipitate a return to classical management and archaic preconceptions [2]. However, an age of re-enlightenment is always possible, wherein aged preconceptions are critically examined for their current and future utility, perhaps delivering the material and spiritual grounds to all of society from which Lean management can then thrive.

The unique aspect of TMS and Lean is the application of scientific thinking (fact or evidence-based thinking) to the practice of management – in addition to its practice on the shop and office floors. These management systems are designed to elicit a determined and relentless focus on causality, causal sequence, and root causes. As such, neither leaders nor workers are afraid of the truth. In classical management, the truth is to be avoided and the preferred understanding of reality is one of make-believe; a make-believe that all is well – that leaders are skilled, employees are doing their jobs just as leaders imagine them to be, suppliers are content, customers are delighted, and that leadership understands and is in full compliance with investors' interests. Appearances are an overriding concern, whether in dreams or in reality.

The scientific method and derivative forms of scientific thinking have long been promoted as the cure for overcoming religion and spirituality. That is a hopeless cause. Both religiosity and spirituality are part of the human condition. However, the latter, secular spirituality, can take forms that promote scientific thinking in ways that are productive to the pursuit of business enterprise, customer satisfaction, and improving human existence. In Toyota's management system, these take the form of PDSA, kaizen, A3 reports, and the seven tools of quality, to name a few.

Like classical management, Lean management possess its own unique spiritual beliefs, mythologies, symbols, and practices. It would be easy to say that Toyota's management system, and its derivative Lean management, are the complete opposite as that described in Chapter 2. But that would not be accurate. The spiritual beliefs pertain more to perceptions than preconceptions and progress in favor of status quo. Lean's spirituality, mysticism, and occult or magical formulations are of a different kind, typically based on accurately perceiving reality and developing wisdom through sensory experiences. Scientific thinking seeks the truth; it destroys what one would prefer to see based on their preconceptions. The truth does not obsequiously submit to tradition or privilege, nor is it shaped by passions, markets, or leaders. Scientific thinking seeks to demystify and understand complex problems, and in the context of TMS, to simplify and continuously improve. In classical management, complex problems fester and simplistic solutions are in abundance. Scientific thinking is cautious, knowing that new truths will emerge with further exploration, while classical management is confident that there is only one truth and no need for further study or experimentation.

In TMS, the teaching of scientific thinking is continuous in supervisor and subordinate relationships and conducted in ways that develops curiosity and utilize human creative potential. For example, you can teach someone how to make a soufflé by following a recipe. That person is a cook. But if the person is taught to understand, through experimentation, all the facts that differentiate good soufflé from bad, the person is more like a food scientist. The person possesses a spirit of inquiry; an insatiable curiosity, like that of a detective, to unravel the mysteries of combinations of ingredients – butter, flour, salt, pepper, milk, eggs (yolk and whites), and cream of tartar, and process – mixing, cookware, temperature, time, atmospheric pressure. It is through such passionate and persistent ground-level work that one discovers the truth. This leads to learning and independent thinking (hypothesis testing) that is applied to other problems.

In TMS, and Lean, this spirit of inquiry, problem-solving through the development of hands-on know-how, is held in the highest regard. It is this spirit that respects people and their ability to generate ideas, create, and innovate. It is this spirit that produces continuous improvement by all employees. Leaders see a moral obligation to develop people so that they can contribute to the betterment of both the company and humanity. In classical management, leaders' preconceptions and associated spirituality murder employees' spirit of inquiry, moral obligations are unseen, and humanity is on its own. The concept and practice of management responsibility are divergent in these two management systems. In TMS, it is based on people, developing human resources, in classical management it is based on money, gain.

So, what do we mean by the spirit of inquiry? What is the

spirituality of TMS and, its derivative Lean management? This is best understood through kaizen – Toyota's kaizen method [3-6]. It is a humanist (other-regarding), not hedonist (self-regarding), habit of using one's curiosity and intelligence to understand and eliminate the problems (abnormalities, or deviations from the normal condition of flow) that cause people to struggle. It means looking at any problem, on the shop and office floor, in any functional area, in any level of the organization, through the lens of an opportunity to discover and learn the truth, and to determine what should be done and quickly bring that to fruition. It means recognizing a problem and taking immediate action to learn the infinite (versus one or two) solutions for improvement. It means teamwork, go see for yourself, get your hands dirty, and making improvements quickly in hours or days, not months or years. It means believing in people; having faith and confidence in the ability of people to think and figure things out on their own.

Figure 3-1 illustrates the spirit of kaizen in the simplest way possible. When a person is encumbered by preconceptions, whether leader or worker, there is only one solution to a problem (top). In TMS and Lean, there are infinite ways to solve the problem (bottom). The number "5" can be taken as a goal, such as improving material or information flow, and there are infinite ways to do that using human ingenuity and creativity – both of which are largely disallowed in classical management, and thus so is continuous improvement (see Note 2). This is a monumental difference in the way of thinking.

$$3 + 2 = \square$$

Classical Management
Preconceptions • One Solution

$$\square + \square = 5$$

Lean Management
Perceptions • Infinite Solutions

Figure 3-1. The top part of the image suggests a boss tells workers what the solution is. The bottom part of the image suggests a boss allows the workers to think for themselves and find their own solutions to the problem. (Image adapted from Toyota Global Knowledge Center training material, 2007).

Problem-solving must be quick and iterative, low cost or no cost, and guided by many other boundary conditions [5] to help people overcome preconceptions and learn how to think differently. Leaders can either train people to comply with their solutions to problems, or leaders can train people how to think and find solutions to the problems that they detect in their own work. When a company moves from classical management to Lean management, people at all levels abandon the enveloping archaic spirituality of the former and adopt the modern, human-centered spirituality of the latter. They abandon preconceptions in favor of sensory perceptions gained at the point where the problem occurs and are trusted to try out their many ideas for improvement.

There is a deep spirituality associated with leaders trusting and respecting workers, and that results in a spiritual connection to one's leaders. People are allowed to ask "Why?," think, and experiment. Creativity in problem-solving produces a higher level of thinking and, through the experience of hundreds and thousands of improvements (taking action) over time, results in the development of wisdom. Those who have developed wisdom possess a deeper relation to the facts (see Note 3), which others with less wisdom can easily see and deeply respect. The spiritual is also embodied in the emotional connections between leaders and followers, each knowing that the other is confident in their knowledge and abilities.

There is also a spiritual connection to the people who teach or facilitate kaizen in the unique forms developed by Toyota [5, 6]. Deeply imbued with the wisdom of people and processes, the sensei (teachers) radiate a spirituality that others deeply respect and absorb. Their teachings span human, technical, and business realms, and they tie everything together so that people understand the meaning of purpose beyond individual or company interests. They help people learn what a problem is, discover the facts, and how to simplify the complex. The simple solutions that teams discover are breathtaking, and it has an emotional impact on them and others. No such thing happens in classical management. Everyone is too busy fighting wars internally and externally.

In TMS and Lean management, a fundamental goal is "survival" in competitive markets, with a strong overtone of togetherness expressed as teamwork and team member.

This differs from the "business as war" mentality, wherein heroic leaders dictate everyone's actions and save the day. The constant, war-like footing means that employees, fearing the worst at any moment, do whatever leaders say and thus do not think about the problems with their own work. Instead, they work around their problems. Survival is a rallying cry for all employees to do what have been trained to do, which is to recognize problems in their own work and quickly develop solutions, every day, and never stop learning to see problems and trying many different ideas to make improvements. It means people think and do, not the boss thinks for you and then you do.

The spiritual ground of classical management is focused on economic, social, and political concerns that subvert people's ability to apply their intelligence to problem-solving. The spiritual ground of Lean management is also focused on economic, social, and political concerns, but in ways that strengthen people's ability to apply their intelligence to problem-solving. Furthermore, the understanding of "respect" and "people" in TMS and Lean management goes beyond the supervisor-subordinate dyad to include suppliers, customers, business partners (joint ventures) investors, and communities. More generally, humanity [7], reflecting a calling higher than mere pecuniary interests.

The amount, quantity, volume, or weight of secular spirituality that accompanies classical management is necessarily huge, given that it is the land of preconceptions and thus make-believe. Leaders must make full use of all available types and forms of secular spirituality to keep everyone focused on pecuniary and other kinds of gain. They help assure that the facts remain forever obscured, at least until a problem becomes so large or threatening that it cannot be ignored by leaders. By then, it is usually too late. Leaders will have breached their fiduciary responsibility to look after the interests of investors and other stakeholders (see Note 4) and are forced to spend large sums of money to correct the problem. Lean management does not guarantee against such outcomes, but their frequency and severity are greatly reduced as a result of having a more accurate view of reality based on the facts.

The spiritual dimensions of TMS and Lean, being mostly tied to exposing facts and being evidence-based, are fundamentally humanist. Consequently, the amount, quantity, volume, or weight of secular spirituality that accompanies TMS and Lean management is necessarily much less. In contrast to make believe, reality reduces the demand on leaders to paint pretty pictures or to confuse people with misleading rhetoric. Being fact-based is one of many forms of respect for people, and people who feel respected are more likely to recognize problems and work together to solve them. It takes continuous teamwork to continuously improve processes. Anyone can improve a process once and move on, as is normally the case in classical management. Under such conditions, process improvement is make-believe and typically done only when ordered by managers – which means, periodically, not continuously. It begs the question, does one really want top managers to think like owners, to be stalwarts of the New

Religion, with all the secular spiritual impedimenta that it entails? Or, would it be better for top managers to think like stewards who understand the facts and make good business decisions on behalf of customers?

The secular spirituality associated with classical management confirms the belief that leaders must establish and maintain firm control. The secular spirituality associated with Lean management recognizes that firm control is difficult to establish and maintain in a chaotic environment – even undesirable. The remedy is to train employees to have the knowledge and capability to adapt quickly to ever-changing circumstances. Leaders who subscribe to classical management are not bad people. They are merely trying to make sense of things and understand the world better, and to feel safe and secure. Leaders who subscribe to Lean management seek to do the same thing. The difference is in how they comprehend reality – through the many preconceptions and the resultant obstruction of learning or mainly through sensory perceptions and the continuous expansion of learning; willingness to managing ever-increasing complexity or motivation to making the complex simple; restraining people's curiosity and initiative or unleashing their ideas and creativity.

TMS and Lean management represent a different economic, social, and political contract between a company and its employees and dependent entities. One that is better able to balance the common but sometimes competing interests between various groups. Business competition should strengthen every individual, not strengthen and leaders and weaken workers. This begs the questions: What is improvement? What is progress?

If traditions and past conventions go unseen, then one can easily claim that progress has been made from one point in time to the next. The technological progress made from 1970 to 2020 is obvious, while economic, social, and political progress may be in arrears. If one is able to see traditions and past conventions, then the claim that progress has been made from one point in time to the next must be qualified. Both improvement and progress will have been restrained by the "dead hand of the past." There is always a conservative fight to retain elements of the past and a progressive alliance to move forward as circumstances change. The result is a failure to keep up with the times in the company, as well as in relation to society's needs and interests. The system for managing people and processes determines the magnitude of the time lag; it is much greater for classical management than for Lean management. The time lag is mostly driven by the concordance between leaders' spiritual and material interests.

––––––––––

The Lean movement's lack of success in persuading top business leaders to replace classical management with Lean management suggests that Lean management is commonly seen as something evil, immoral, or a cause of suffering that is capable of destroying their way of life, the corporate way of life, and possibly society. Rational arguments have failed in part because Lean advocates have not acknowledged the importance of secular spirituality in helping leaders understand their job and the conduct of business. No matter how much evidence there is, it is not enough to get leaders to cross the chasm from classical management to Lean management. The gap between the believers of one management system and the believers of another management system cannot be closed by reasoning because the obstruction is spiritual in nature – and people, leaders or workers, are loath to give that up. The spirituality of Lean management is foreign and exotic and more challenging than that which is long familiar, even though it may be deficient. Rather than being seen as a better way, Lean management and its quest to understand the causal sequence of problems, is seen as despiritualizing people, confusing the truth, subverting authority, and provoking disunity.

The professional class of Lean advocates does not recognize that leaders have the right to ignore the facts. They have long over-relied on the strength of reason and evidence. Nevertheless, they press forward despite not understanding, in the requisite detail, why leaders dislike Lean management. Their faith in Lean management interferes with their ability to discern the truth of these circumstances. For example, Lean management puts certain limits on leaders' authority and gives workers greater say in how work should be performed. The evidence over the past 30-plus years indicates that, in general, neither leaders nor workers find this to be appealing. The materialist results of the status quo, as well as its secular spiritual underpinnings, are good enough for both. Business leaders have little use for new thinking or agents of change whose ideas impinge upon them or their work. The spiritual basis for ameliorating this perspective has not been established for leaders or workers. Therefore, neither will seek anything better. Instead, business leaders' reasonable approach is to adopt parts of Lean management, selected tools and methods, for workers to use. This cooperative decision-making choice adequately fulfills the moral and fiduciary duties of leadership, and to maintain appearances among their peers.

Business leaders are widely known to be conservative, consistently over hundreds of years. They dislike technocratic solutions to problems in social organizations of any type or size. Anything that has the appearance of perfecting people or society robs them of their freedom and individuality and saps the economy of needed energy and enterprise. From their perspective, technocratic solutions such as Lean management weaken, not strengthen, and are dead on arrival. Conservative business values have deep spiritual and material meanings, and are seen as well-tailored to the task of meeting the competitive challenges of the marketplace and fending off attacks from rivals.

Yet, the Lean movement continues along the path established long ago to gain a greater following, under some mystical or spiritual belief that the methods used – focused on evidence and reason – will eventually gain a following among CEOs and hourly workers. There is also an enduring mystical fascination about changing leaders' behaviors, and that with more intense focus and more facts the desired changes in behaviors will follow. Perhaps persistence will pay. But progress comes more rapidly when problems are understood in finer levels of detail. Absent that, influential Lean promoters dispense guidance and offer diversions that maintains the status quo, thus causing people to suspend their thinking as to why leaders don't want to manage business more scientifically.

Figure 3-2 helps put matters into perspective. Classical management was established hundreds of years ago, and some elements of its practice go back thousands of years. In contrast, modern progressive management systems are recent developments. They have existed for the last 110 years or so, and all carry forward a similar theme of continuous process improvement and the sustained training and development of both managers and workers. The habits of mind, both spiritual and material, have yet to be

System	Established
Classical Management (System of Profound Privilege)	Centuries Ago (and longer)
Scientific Management	1911
Toyota Management	1973
Lean Management	1988
Dr. Deming's System of Profound Knowledge	1990

Figure 3-2. Modern progressive management systems are new, within the last 110 years or so, while classical management has been around for much longer.

established in society for Lean management. In contrast, the spiritual and material habits of mind for classical management have long been in place and are thus firmly established. As a result, these habits of mind, for leaders and workers alike, are very difficult to change except in isolated cases – meaning, small numbers of companies of any size or in any industry.

Figure 3-2 suggests that the advancement and more widespread adoption of Lean management will take more than one hundred years. It is a multi-century transition, not a 32-year project. The scope of acceptance asked for Lean management has been beyond what is possible. Change takes place over very long periods of time, periodically accelerated by one or two major economic, social, or political events that soften traditional rigid thinking followed by a gradual drift towards a new and stronger understanding. As these pages show, as well as those in *The Triumph of Classical Management* and *Irrational Institutions*, there are robust forces working against Lean management that have yet to exhaust themselves. Leaders' opinions or assertions against Lean management carry more weight than all the totality of fact-based evidence in favor of Lean management. Even successful Lean CEOs have great difficulty influencing their peers, in large part because they are deeply skeptical of the value of scientific thinking as applied to leadership and management.

These and other facts go unrecognized, unappreciated, or ignored in pursuit of the business of Lean management. Over the decades, TMS and Lean have spawned thousands of companies offering many forms of consulting, training, and other services, with qualifications ranging from smooth talker to experienced and knowledgeable doer. Everyone claims great success on their web site and in marketing materials, but the reality is that while magnificent revenues may have been generated jointly or severally, the impact on client organizations is usually small or non-existent. Business leaders prefer that outcome, recognizing that such services are more for the purpose of invidious comparison (who has the most expensive consultant; see Note 5), maintaining appearances, or avoiding the role of the pacesetter. The principal point seems to be to display how much money leaders can waste on eliminating waste. The material outcome, overall, is nugatory, but the spiritual need has been amply fulfilled.

Yet, the business of Lean continues apace, perhaps now being more important than Lean management itself, embodying all of the essential values of business materiality and spirituality. For some, Lean management is a consequential profession and for others it is an enchanting hobby. As with anything today that attains some level of popularity, Lean has a bountiful presence on social media, replete with the requisite fads (kata), ceremonies (group photos), cliques (in-group members and those that have been blocked), and sainthood for the preeminent. The talk is mostly among one another, given top leaders' disinterest in Lean management, with much discussion of benefits that many have seen or heard but few have themselves created. The true believers are undeterred, happily so as the long fight wears on, and remain true to their icons. As such, Lean has become a type of religion which, predictably, leads to arguments aplenty between the straight and true and the uninformed and debasing imitators. Much of this is needed and healthy debate in search of sense-making and progress. Though, quite a few have claimed Lean management's followers to be members of a cult, given that Lean seems to promise much but has delivered little. Characteristics of a cult include:

- Leader is infallible or omniscient
- Critical inquiry is rejected
- Members are penalized or ostracized
- Demand for loyalty and devotion
- Exploitation or abuse of group members
- Generating fear or hostility
- Us versus them mentality

There are collective behaviors that have the flavor of a cult and seem excessive and unhealthy. Lean movement leaders are idolized as prophets, complete with a vocal coterie eager to defend them against any criticism of their work. There is a prevailing view that only the ideas and methods that come from Toyota, or sound like they come from Toyota, are worthy. These reflect a lack of independent thinking common to cults (and fads). Adoration of the idol, Toyota (Figure 3-3), is sometimes used perniciously to competitively rank one's Lean credibility or superiority, despite, perhaps, having little actual experience with it. This moves past the intended material realm of practical, hands-on action to develop one's self and improve processes to the spiritual realm of fantasy and superstition.

Figure 3-3. Lean people worshipping at the Toyota totem, the venerated symbol of true Lean management.

One's employment should consist of two things: doing the job and improving the job. That should be true no matter if one is a member of the Board of Directors, the CEO, or a shop or office floor worker. Doing both encompasses the reality that times change, people have ideas, and people want to apply their intellect to creative and innovative ends. Employment should not be a hinderance to that. The difficulty is in understanding what improvement is. The Toyota Way of thinking and doing leads to creative breakthroughs that are of a fundamentally different nature, and therefore stands superior to how improvement is understood in classical management. Furthermore, in classical management, the usual workers' focus is limited to doing the job because leaders disable their interest and abilities to improve their job. And, as classical management is conservative and incurious in its orientation, most leaders have near-zero interest in improving their job. That sets the example.

The epigram commonly heard in organizations, "the more things change, the more they stay the same" [8], is the result of employees laboring under a static spirituality and materialism that has long since passed and does not reflect the humanism that is needed for this century and beyond (see Note 6).

Questions to Reflect On

- Referring to Figure 3-3, do you think the people in the image are seeing the bigger picture? Why or why not?

- Progressive management has been around for about 110 years. What would a survival plan for the next 200 years look like?

- What should the Lean movement do to establish the spiritual basis for Lean in society?

- If CEOs listen only to other CEOs, what can successful Lean CEOs do differently to be heard? What can successful Lean CEOs do differently to influence shop and office floor laborers in other organizations?

- Which management practice do you believe is better at preserving or improving your social and economic interests: classical management or Lean management? Explain why.

- It often seems as if knowing about Lean management is more important than tenaciously practicing Lean, giving the impression of widespread "Lean hobbyism." Meaning, a satisfaction with the status quo among the Lean professional staff; a progressive sentiment that does not translate into broader action. What can the professional staff do differently to produce a more encompassing sense of obligation to one another and social connectedness through the shared understanding and practice of Lean management?

- Does Lean management have a future in a digitized business world? Make the case for and against.

Notes

1. Prior to automobile manufacturing, Toyoda was in the loom manufacturing and spinning and weaving businesses. These businesses competed globally in free markets. See *Toyota: A History of the First 50 Years*, Toyota Motor Corporation, Toyota City, Japan, 1988, pp. 23-48 and K. Wada and T. Yui, *Courage and Change: The Life of Kiichiro Toyoda*, Toyota Motor Corporation, Toyota City, Japan, 2002, pp. 109-190

2. In defending the value of the MBA degree, the dean of Northwestern University's Kellogg School of Management, Dr. Francesca Cornelli, said: "This is a collaborative space, a safe space where you can stretch yourself, take risks. You can't experiment or stretch [like that] on the job." She's right. Classical management discourages experimentation in the workplace. See Thomas, P. (2020), "Kellogg Dean Says M.B.A.'s Future is Uncertain, and That's All Right," *The Wall Street Journal*, 4 March, https://www.wsj.com/articles/kellogg-dean-says-m-b-a-s-future-is-uncertain-and-thats-all-right-11583326800

3. In TPS and Lean management, facts are treated as impersonal objects. In classical management, facts are treated as animistic objects that threaten a person's power, prestige, rights, and privileges. Facts exert a powerful negative social and political effect on people, especially leaders, whose habit of mind is mediated by animism. Instead of impersonal or inert cause and effect, they imagine personal forces of good or evil, merit or demerit, safety or

threat, convention or change. When this happens, the facts are ignored, and improvement is delayed or does not take place unless it is expedient in terms of business (and corporeal property) need. When facts are treated as mere objects, then then improvement can take place whenever and wherever it is needed – and it is not restricted to business (or corporeal property) need. The difference in how facts are treated in classical versus Lean management also foretells the levels of curiosity exhibited by leaders. It is often stated by business leaders and in surveys completed by leaders that curiosity is one of the most important leadership traits; adaptability, tolerance of ambiguity, and openness to differences being other important traits – all are untrue for most leaders (a fantasy; part of the mythology of leadership). However, it is clear that curiosity runs on two different planes for classical management compared to Lean management. In the former, curiosity runs on the low plane of the superficial, if not trivial or frivolous, while in the latter curiosity runs on the higher plane of being a matter of survival and is therefore of utmost importance.

4. If business leaders don't look after other stakeholders' interests such as employees (Boeing 737 Max), customers (Wells Fargo fraud), suppliers (Baxter's heparin contamination), and communities (Vale mining dam disaster), then, *ipso facto*, investors interests will be harmed. This highlights a significant flaw in leaders' usual understanding of the New Religion.

5. It is honorific and a measure of one's status to hire a prominent and expensive consultant. Competitors, relying

on glittery reputation, mystically believe that the parties are expertly executing changes that will yield sustainable competitive advantage. In most cases, the changes become diluted or fall away upon the return to business as usual.

6. If you were to ask a dying person what they will miss the most, other than family and friends or pets, their answer would likely be the things that gave them the most pleasure such as cooking, reading, nature, films, television, gardening, sports, theater, music, dance, paintings, and so on. Mostly, the arts. If you were to ask the dying person what they will miss the least, their answer would likely be the things that have annoyed them the most, such as their former managers. Management is not an art, and neither is leadership, because, typically, more people disapprove than approve of them. For the arts to be enjoyable, the artist must be aware of and understand causality (gap between plan and actual or between vision and execution; i.e. feedback) as they develop and improve the skills needed to produce their art. In classical management, leaders and managers, largely ignore causality, so they are, in general, perpetually unskilled and thus unable to consistently produce pleasurable experiences for others. It should be further noted that the archaic definition of "management" is "trickery" and "deceit," and as *Management Mysterium* has shown, as well as *The Triumph of Classical Management* and *Irrational Institutions*, this archaic definition is alive and well in business today.

References

[1] Toyota (1988), *Toyota: A History of the First 50 Years,* Toyota Motor Corporation, Toyota City, Japan, pp. 95-96.

[2] Emiliani, B., Stec., D., Grasso, L., and Stodder, J. (2007), *Better Thinking, Better Results: Case Study and Analysis of an Enterprise-Wide Lean Transformation,* Second Edition, The CLBM, LLC, Wethersfield, Conn.

[3] Kato, I. and Smalley, A. (2011), *Toyota Kaizen Methods: Six Steps to Improvement,* CRC Press, Boca Raton, Florida

[4] Narusawa, T. and Shook, J. (2009), *Kaizen Express: Fundamentals for Your Lean Journey,* Lean Enterprise Institute, Cambridge, Mass.

[5] Emiliani, B., Yoshino, K., and Go, R. (2015), *Kaizen Forever: Teachings of Chihiro Nakao,* The CLBM, LLC, Wethersfield, Conn.

[6] Wood, R., Herscher, M., and Emiliani, B. (2015), *Shingijutsu-Kaizen: The Art of Discovery and Learning,* The CLBM, LLC, Wethersfield, Conn.

[7] For more on the "Respect for People" and "Respect for Humanity" principle, see Michel Baudin's blog https://michelbaudin.com/2013/05/08/this-respect-for-people-stuff/ and https://michelbaudin.com/2014/04/12/more-on-toyotas-respect-for-humanity/

[8] The epigram is attributed to Jean-Baptiste Alphonse Karr circa 1848: "Plus ça change, plus c'est la même chose." https://en.wikipedia.org/wiki/Jean-Baptiste_Alphonse _Karr

4
Conclusion

"All facts of observation are necessarily seen in the light of the observer's habits of thought, and the most intimate and inveterate of his habits of thought is the experience of his own initiative and endeavours."

- Thorstein Veblen

Conclusion

The Triumph of Classical Management, *Irrational Institutions*, and *Management Mysterium* are not the usual boosterism for Lean that one finds. Instead, these books challenge Lean promoters and advocates to a sobering recognition that their cause, important as it may be, is much more difficult than they understand or imagine. It is wise for readers to look skeptically at the those who promote Lean management and gain a better understanding of the facts about it and learn why leaders don't share their enthusiasm. The more knowledge one gains, the more likely it is that new ideas will be generated that help overcome or circumvent barriers, notwithstanding events that may soften leaders' commitment to classical management.

In this book, I have ventured to show how and why secular spirituality exists, how it functions, and what it achieves in the narrow context of classical management and Lean management. We have seen how remnants from the Middle Ages remains with us today, hundreds of years later, and how they still hold great power and influence in the domains of economics and classical management. Secular spirituality is conjoined to the practice of both leadership and management in all its forms. It can perpetuate the status quo or be used to support change and improvement. It can dictate one solution or illuminate infinite solutions. It can hide facts or expose facts. It can instill fear or erase fear. It can stifle thinking or liberate creativity. It can suppress knowledge or expose the truth. It can subdue people or enliven and engage people.

The analyses presented also venture to show how classical management is no longer right for the times we live in. Its archaic preconceptions hold back the progress of individuals, organizations, and society. Unfortunately, reason does not go nearly as far as one would hope in convincing leaders to abandon classical management. Perhaps it is most important to recognize that material and spiritual grounds of classical management are still in the process of being strengthened (see Note 1). The spiritual and material grounds for progressive management have only recently been laid, and they encompass only a microscopic portion of society. There remains much more work to do over the upcoming century or two, assuming Lean management or future variations remain relevant to human existence. Either way, now is the time to lead a new movement, the Age of Re-Enlightenment, to move past archaic ideas whose time has long passed (see Note 2).

The inhuman or less human shape of classical management reflects a static moribund traditionalism that no longer serves its purpose. In contrast, Lean management – management with a human touch – reflects an energetic, living framework whose fundamental ideas and methods are continuously subject to review and modification for the purpose of improvement, made in-time. The secular spiritualism associated with classical management is a continuous blessing of the New Religion, economics, handed down from the Middle Ages. Leaders are weary of theories of unbelief such as Lean management. One can easily understand their perspective, but leaders' everlasting collective drive for group-preservation and unbridled gain is incontestably pathological.

Yet, time passes and individuals and society change. Eventually, leaders may tire or see things differently [1-3] and allow needed changes. They will adjust, reluctantly at first, and perhaps soon realize that they have gained more than they lost. The rights and privileges that have so long been part of their tradition may not be so important after all. They may come to appreciate the values and ideals of workmanship, which mature and reward the spirit, mind, and body. They may also find a calmer inner life that delimits the drive for material gain, yet still be our cherished winners.

Then again, maybe not.

I am always interested to hear from readers because I learn new things. Tell me what you think of this book, *The Triumph of Classical Management*, or *Irrational Institutions*. Let's make arrangements to have a conversation by phone or Skype. You pick the topic. Contact me at bob@bobemiliani.com.

Questions to Reflect On

- What are your key takeaways from this book pertaining to Chapters 1, 2, and 3?

- In what ways did this book change your thinking?

- Is there anything you learned that you could apply to your work or to advance Lean management?

- What aspects of this book do you like or agree with, or dislike or disagree with?

- Create a table comparing the secular spiritual features of classical management to Lean management. What does it reveal in relation to pragmatism and humanism?

- Will future leaders tire or see things differently and allow needed changes? Make the case for and against.

- Will leaders be driven to preserve their reputation and legitimacy ("conceit of pride") based on past successes and traditions, or will they be willing to sacrifice the old for the new? Make the case for and against.

Notes

1. Someday soon, artificial intelligence (AI) will move from prediction to decision-making or recommending decisions for human leaders to make. How will leaders react to machine-made decisions or recommendations? Will they accept them uncritically, as-is, incuriously? That is the easiest way. Or, will they inquire as to the machine's assumptions or reasoning? That could cause confusion. Will leaders go see the problem first-hand to verify the adequacy of the decision? That has not been their traditional habit of mind. Once a decision is made, who will monitor, verify, or correct the outcome? And what about fairness? Will machine-generated decisions and recommendations be fair and free of bias? It seems likely that pressure to produce AI systems and machines that are capable of making decisions will follow the basic patterns of business logic that have been established since the Middle Ages because, to the unknowing mind, what has served humanity well in the past is undoubtedly useful for the future. Is there any need to question this?

2. Idea distancing.

References

[1] Jaben, M. (2019), *Free the Brain: Overcome the Struggle People and Organizations Face with Change*, Egbert Publishing

[2] Pinker, S. (2018), *Enlightenment Now: The Case for Reason, Science, Humanism, and Progress*, Penguin Books, New York, New York

[3] Harari, Y. (2019), *21 Lessons for the 21ˢᵗ Century*, Spiegel & Grau, New York, New York

NOTES

NOTES

About the Author

M.L. "Bob" Emiliani is a professor in the School of Engineering, Science, and Technology at Connecticut State University in New Britain, Conn., where he teaches a course on leadership, a unique course that analyzes failures in management decision-making, as well as other courses.

Bob earned a Bachelor of Science degree in mechanical engineering from the University of Miami, a Master of Science degree in chemical engineering from the University of Rhode Island, and a Doctor of Philosophy degree in Engineering from Brown University.

He worked in the consumer products and aerospace industries for 15 years, beginning as a materials engineer. He has held management positions in engineering, manufacturing, and supply chain management at Pratt & Whitney.

Bob joined academia in September 1999. While in academia, he developed the Lean teaching pedagogy and led activities to continuously improve master's degree programs.

Emiliani has authored or co-authored 22 books, four book chapters, and more than 45 peer-reviewed papers. He has received six awards for writing.

Please visit www.bobemiliani.com

.

www.ingramcontent.com/pod-product-compliance
Lightning Source LLC
Chambersburg PA
CBHW031946190326
41519CB00007B/678